KU-487-175

FOLLOW THROUGH

A Second Teacher's Handbook of Stories and Themes from the Bible

Written for the Association of
Christian Teachers Scotland by

J. C. Currie
C. P. Johnston
D. MacCuish
J. G. Muir
C. M. Rose

Illustrations by Margaret Shearer

BLACKIE

Blackie & Son Ltd
Bishopbriggs
Glasgow G64 2NZ

7 Leicester Place
London WC2H 7BP

Acknowledgments
We are extremely grateful to Mrs Pamela Macdonald for painstakingly
typing out the edited manuscript for us over several months.
We are also grateful to Dr D. M. McFarlan for permission to adapt for
inclusion here his text on Psalms and Proverbs from his book
Who? What? Where? in the Bible.

© ACT Scotland 1985

First published 1985
ISBN 0 216 91735 2

All Rights Reserved
No part of this publication may be reproduced,
stored in a retrieval system, or transmitted,
in any form or by any means,
electronic, mechanical, photocopying, recording or otherwise,
without prior permission of Blackie & Son Ltd

Printed and bound in Great Britain by
McCorquodale (Scotland) Ltd.

PREFACE

Follow Through is a sequel to *Start Here* which was written for teachers of younger children. In this book we have selected stories and themes from the Old and New Testament which are suitable for children in the age range 8–13. We hope it will provide teachers with the basis for a meaningful R.E. programme. In each case the biblical source is quoted. Even teachers who have little or no knowledge of the Bible can use the stories by reading the relevant passages beforehand, preferably in a modern version such as the *Good News Bible*.

It is not meant to replace other approaches. We recognize that teachers will wish to include in their wider programme a consideration of faiths other than Christianity. There are many useful and easily obtainable publications which deal with these.

At the beginning we list the stories both in order of the book and also grouped in themes. The lessons can be done in the order in which they appear or they can be introduced through the themes suggested at the appropriate times in the year. The time taken for each lesson will depend on the amount of work the teacher plans to do, but for those who wish to develop the stories further, either in class or assembly, we have included a number of optional related activities with simple, easy-to-follow sketches for guidance where appropriate.

Because these lessons have been written for a wide age range, it will be necessary for teachers to select and adapt them, according to the age and ability of their own class.

USEFUL PUBLICATIONS AND PUBLISHERS

We list here some of the books which we use most frequently in our lessons. Not all are still in print but may be found in the resource library.

HYMNS, SONGS AND PRAYERS

1. *The Church Hymnary*, Third Edition   (O.U.P.)
2. *Someone's Singing, Lord*   (Black)
3. *Carol, Gaily Carol*   (Black)
4. *Merrily to Bethlehem*   (Black)
5. *Apusskidu*   (Black)
6. *Sing to God*   (Scripture Union)
7. *Come and Praise*   (B.B.C. Publications)
8. *Youth Praise* 1 and 2   (Falcon Books; Church Pastoral Aid Society)

BIBLE STORIES AND CHARACTERS

1. Ladybird Books
2. Lion Publications
3. Scripture Union Publications
4. Religious and Moral Education Press Publications
5. 'Read About It' series   (Wheaton)
6. National Bible Society Publications for Children
7. Frances Hook *Present Day Pictures*   (N.C.E.C.)
8. *Start Here*   (Blackie)
9. *The Nazarene File*   (Blackie)
10. The 'Getting to know about . . .' series—*In the Lands of the Bible* (Denholm House Press, N.C.E.C.)
11. Bible News series of cassettes of bible events in 'news' format (Bible News Publications)

GENERAL REFERENCE

1. *Who? What? Where? in the Bible*   (Blackie)
2. *Behold the Land*—Pictorial Atlas   (Philip)
3. *The Lion Encyclopaedia of the Bible*   (Lion)
4. *The New English Study Bible*   (Holmes McDougall)
5. Blackwell's Learning Library
6. *Religious Education, Primary School Handbook*   (Scottish Joint Committee on Religious Education)
7. *Living Light*   (Holmes McDougall)
8. The How and Why Books   (Transworld)
9. *Learning About Religion*   (Schofield and Sims)
10. *Life in Bible Times*   (Chambers)

CONTENTS

A THEMATIC APPROACH USING THE STORIES SELECTED

OLD TESTAMENT

THE CREATION STORY

Genesis 1–3

AIM

To give an account of the biblical story of creation and to encourage children to appreciate the world and the part they can play in it.

NOTE: In an age when there is controversial scientific debate about the origins of the world, some teachers may feel that there is no place for the creation story as told in the Bible. We feel, however, that the early chapters of Genesis introduce a religious dimension to the discussion and it should be borne in mind that the account was not written as a science textbook but as a story relevant to all ages. It is basically a simple attempt to give a reason for the world's existence and an explanation of the relationship between God and man. It will continue to be hotly debated even among Christians and for this reason also we feel that it is important that children are familiar with it.

INTRODUCTION

"Beginnings" may be talked about, leading on to man's constant quest to find his "roots". This generally goes beyond research into one's ancestors, for man often wishes to know what purpose he has in life. Teachers may debate the pros and cons of the various theories of evolution (and there are quite a few) or simply give the Bible account of the beginning of the world and man in particular. Read over the first few chapters of Genesis for yourself before taking the lesson.

SUGGESTED PROCEDURE

1. (Genesis 1:1–31) Explain that in the book of Genesis there is an account of how the world began (why and how man was made and the reasons for the existence of good and bad). We are told that God made the earth, the seas, plants, the sun to shine during the day and the moon to provide a lesser light at night. Relate to science lessons on the cycle of the seasons. Finally, after the creation of birds and animals, God made man. The account says that God was pleased with all that he had made.

2. The first chapter (from verse 26) goes on to explain that God made man, called Adam, to look after all that he had created. The Bible speaks about a garden but it is probably worth explaining that it is likely that this was a very large area, with four rivers running through it. The last act of creation was God's provision of a friend and companion for Adam, a woman whom he called Eve. God told them that they could live in the beautiful world which he had created and could eat what they wished of all the fruit and herbs that were provided except fruit from one tree.

3. In Genesis 3:1–7 we read that God's enemy came to them in the form of a snake and persuaded Eve to take the forbidden fruit, telling her that this would give them knowledge like God's which was why God did not want them to eat it! She believed him and they both ate the fruit.

4. Emphasize not so much the substance of the fruit, but the fact that they had disobeyed. This changed their relationship with God which had been based on trust and honesty. Now, for the first time, they experienced fear and shame, so they hid from God. Naturally it is hard to hide from God! He found them and expressed his disappointment with them, then banished them from the beautiful land he had given them. From then on they had to work and toil for themselves in less fertile ground, where they would have to plough, sow, weed and reap among thorns and thistles to make a living in a hostile world.

5. The narrative ends here but go on to discuss the many beautiful things in God's world, the majesty and wonder of mountains, rivers, lakes and valleys; the beauty of plants and animals. (Reference might be made to the points raised in "God's Wonderful World" in *Start Here*.) Talk about the complexity of the simplest insect or a tiny snowflake. Speak also about time and the seasons and the vastness of the universe with its patterns of stars and planets so perfectly ordered that for centuries man has plotted their cycles. Discuss what we can do to show our appreciation of the world around us.

How do you feel

1. When you **want** to do wrong?
2. When you **do** wrong?

6. Consider some of the things which make man similar to many of the other animals and emphasize the factors which make him a unique creation. "God created human beings, making them to be like himself" (Genesis 1:27).
   (a) His ability to control many plants and animals.
   (b) The responsibility which he has with this power.
   (c) The skills which he can acquire, and above all teach others, to create beautiful things.
   (d) The ability to think, feel, love and be loved.
   (e) The ability to love and follow God.
7. It is important also to speak about the evil and wrongdoing which man perpetuates throughout the world. Reference might be made simply to a newspaper or television bulletin.
8. Conclude by discussing the personal choices which each of us often has between good and bad, right and wrong, and our responsibility to consider other people. It is this ability to choose between right and wrong, the essence of the creation story, which makes us unique. The main point of the creation story is that God did not make us as robots, programmed to do as we are told, but gave us minds to think and bodies to act.

CLASS ROBOT

Feels
thinks
sees
creates
smells
hears
talks

CLASS MAN

OPTIONAL ACTIVITIES

1. A sense of the wonder of creation can be evoked (as in *Start Here*) through an environmental study topic. Reference to the plants, animals, the heavens and the seas can be related to the creation story if desired.
2. Stories from everyday life about choices between good and bad could be told or written. You may wish to reflect on what makes our conscience as it is and consider aspects such as parents' standards, school standards, rules and regulations, church attendance or belief in God. Some older children can discuss this very seriously.
3. Sing: "God who made the earth" or "For the beauty of the earth" or "All things bright and beautiful" or "Think of a world without any flowers".
4. Children could make up a suitable prayer related to our respect for God's creation, our obedience to his truths, and asking for strength to do what is right.
5. Using colour slides make up a tape/slide presentation of the story.
6. Discuss the work of the Nature Conservancy and similar organizations.

"GOOD done by man...."

EVIL done by man

Layers of paper to give 3D look
Pale blue sky: dark purple mts:
dark green hills: light green grass:
Tweed for tree trunks: tissue for
foliage: brown for animals and
bright yellow paper for people.

(Frieze size or smaller)

ABRAHAM

INTRODUCTORY NOTE

Abraham, founder of the Jewish race, shining example of the man of faith and friend of God, lived about 2000 B.C. in Mesopotamia, the land between the Rivers Tigris and Euphrates.

Ur of the Chaldees, a prosperous city of sturdy houses, was dominated by a great ziggurat built in honour of the moon-god, one of the many gods worshipped in that land. From this civilized city Abraham was called by God to set out on a lifetime of wandering, living in tents like the despised barbarians. He obeyed the call, not knowing where he was to go but confident that God would be with him.

For many long years Abraham was without an heir, although God had promised him a son. As the story unfolds we shall see how his faith was tested.

The story of Abraham (with his weaknesses as well as his strengths) is, in a sense, a real-life parable and, like all parables, may live in the memory provoking thought intermittently over the years.

ABRAHAM

Lesson 1   Destination Unknown

Genesis 11:27–32; 12:1–10; 13:1–4

AIM

1. To introduce the children to an important Old Testament character.
2. To show Abraham's trust in God and, implicitly, something of the nature of trust.

INTRODUCTION

Spend some time on the theme of journeys, e.g.
1. Journeys taken by the children.
2. Moving house.
3. Journeys in the news.

Talk (or write) about these aspects:
1. Before the journey—preparations, finding out where they're going, feelings (of apprehension, anticipation, excitement), goodbyes, last look round.
2. The journey—means of transport, pleasures and pains, length, time taken.
3. The arrival—feelings of relief, happiness, achievement.

SUGGESTED PROCEDURE

1. Display pictures and a map of Mesopotamia. Also useful would be a large sketch map on which to trace the journey to Canaan.
2. Tell the story of Abraham's journey focusing on these points:
   (a) Abraham's life in Ur where he lived with his beautiful wife, Sarah.

THEN ...
and NOW!

Introduce his old father, Terah, brother Nahor and nephew Lot. Tell about the ziggurats and multiplicity of gods.

(b) His decision to leave Ur and why. He had been aware of God speaking to him, urging him to leave his homeland and set out for a land which he would show him.
(Have they ever had a friend come to them whispering, "Come till I show you something"? It shows you that you're his friend and it's exciting.)
God promised him three things:
(i) To show him a land.
(ii) To take care of him. Emphasize what a great undertaking the journey was. Ask the children what misgivings he might have had, e.g. friends (and his brother) left behind, dangers on the way (enemies, hunger, thirst), lack of comforts.
(iii) To give him a big family—he would have children, grand-children, and great-grandchildren till there would be thousands and thousands of descendants.

(c) Preparations and goodbyes. It was quite a caravan that set out—Abraham, Sarah, Lot, servants, animals, tents, household utensils, etc.
(d) The journey—on camel, donkey and foot; setting up camp; possible adventures.
(e) The arrival in Haran where they settled for five years—possibly because the old grandfather couldn't go any further, or he may have had connections with the place. When he died they resumed their journey once more.
(f) Eventual arrival in Canaan. Describe the land—densely wooded land of mountains, rivers and lush, flower-strewn pastures. It was a good land that God had shown him. However, there were already people living there. But God had something to tell Abraham—one day that land would belong to his descendants! (God had kept his promise—he'd taken care of them and led them to the promised land.)

OPTIONAL ACTIVITIES

1. Writing: At some point before the land of Canaan is reached the class could write a composite poem on the theme "Show me a land". Each child should write down what he or she would like to see (or hear) there;
"Show me a land where . . ."
and the various suggestions should then be arranged into a poem. Illustrate the poem.
2. Read Genesis 12:1–5 to the class.

7

3. Hymn: Sing "God has promised" or "One more step along the way I go" *(Come and Praise)*

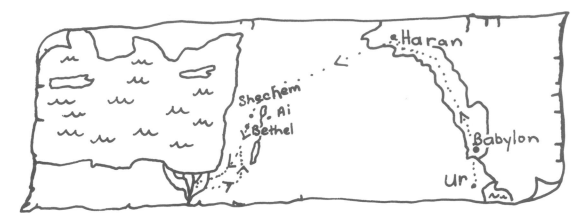

4. Find Israel on a map of the Middle East and trace the journey on the sketch map referred to above, e.g. Illustration in *Good News Bible*.
5. Mime/act some of the incidents on the theme of journeys.
6. Share stories and poems from other sources on the same theme.

Lesson 2   A Quarrel

Genesis 13 : 5–18

AIM

1. To tell the story of Abraham's generous dealing with his nephew, Lot.
2. To give an example of a sensible way of handling a disagreement.

INTRODUCTION

Briefly recapitulate the story so far. Alternatively, let the class talk about their experiences of quarrelling with the frequent misery entailed.

SUGGESTED PROCEDURE

Tell the story, emphasizing the following main points:
1. The quarrel between the two groups of herdsmen. Both Abraham and his nephew were prosperous with no lack of sheep, goats, camels, silver, gold. The herdsmen began to quarrel. The children might suggest bones of contention, e.g.
   "That's where our sheep are going!"
   "Hey, you've used all the water!"
   "We were here first!", etc.
2. Abraham's offer. There is a selfishness/generosity issue here and it should be made explicit.
   (a) Who gets first choice? As the older man Abraham might have expected to have it.
   (b) After Abraham's generous offer Lot had the chance to be generous in turn—and failed to take it.

(c) God's reiterated promise to Abraham (Genesis 13:14–18): "I am going to give you and your descendants all the land that you can see and it will be yours forever."

OPTIONAL ACTIVITIES

1. Act out the story. Since there can be any number of servants and herdsmen the whole class could well take part.
2. Discuss further experiences of quarrelling among friends or between nations.

Lesson 3   A Son for Abraham and Sarah

Genesis 15:1–7; 17:1–8; 18:1–15; 21:1–8

AIM

1. To show that Abraham kept on believing that God would give him a son.
2. To show that God keeps his promises though there may be a long delay.
3. To help build up a picture of the semi-nomadic life of the time.

INTRODUCTION

Recall the promises God made to Abraham back in Ur.
1. The land—he has arrived!
2. God's care—they've been protected and have prospered.
3. An heir—still, after all these years they have no son.

SUGGESTED PROCEDURE

1. Describe their life as semi-nomads moving from camp-site to camp-site in search of fresh pasture.
   Their large brown striped tents made of woven goat's hair usually had a separate "room" curtained off at the back for the women. It was they who were responsible for setting up the tents and for the "housekeeping".

crushed paper

cold water paste

ball paste on squares on dry ball

neck of roll of cereal packet card to fit forefinger.

fix on head

add on features

press hollows for eyes

Cover with layer of small 1" pieces cheap toilet paper.

wool strips tied in middle for hair

PUPPETS OF ABRAHAM & LOT!!

Food was reasonably varied—there were fruits, meat, bread, butter, milk, cheese, honey and even coffee (but no sugar or tea!).

Point out that Abraham and Sarah were prosperous and happy—except for one thing. Can the children say what is still lacking? Bring out the fact that year after year had passed and still they had no son. Had God forgotten his promise?

JIGSAWS

HOME WORK

Leisure LOVE

MONEY Friends

What's Missing?

2. *The Promise Reiterated*

Tell how one night Abraham was outside the tent looking up at the dark sky full of stars. It was as if God said, "Count the stars Abraham" and Abraham said, "I can't; there are so many—millions and millions of them." Then God said, "You'll have a son Abraham, and he'll have children. They will grow up and have children and there will be grandchildren and there will be great-grandchildren and so on till the end of time. There will be thousands and thousands of them just as there are thousands and thousands of stars". Abraham believed God and God was pleased with him because he did. It showed that Abraham trusted God. Abraham was a friend of God.

3. *The Passage of Years*

Still no child. It looked as if God had forgotten.

SHEEP FARMERS JOURNAL

Births

4. *Three Mysterious Visitors* (Genesis 18:1–16).

This scene gives a vivid picture of Eastern hospitality and is worth describing in detail.

(a) Abraham at the tent door, Sarah busy inside.

(b) The welcome—Abraham ran to meet them, bowed and brought water for their feet. (Compare to our standard "cup of tea" welcome.)

(c) The meal—of veal, butter, milk and cakes. Describe the preparation of the meal. The cakes would be made from a mixture of flour and milk and baked on a hearth of stones. The visitors were served in the shade of a tree.

(d) Their message for Sarah: "She shall have a son." Her incredulity evokes the response, "Is anything too hard for the Lord?"

Honey butter

coffee cheese

bread

5. *The Promised Son*

One year later their baby was born. Do any of the children know the name he was given? (Isaac). Describe their joy and how they felt more sure than ever that God was their friend. He had kept all his promises.

OPTIONAL ACTIVITIES

1. The children could tell the story from the point of view of either Abraham or Sarah.

2. Sing: "God has promised" (*Come and Praise*).

3. Write: "Is anything too hard for the Lord?" in beautiful writing. Do it on pastel-coloured paper and decorate the edges.

SARAH

ISAAC

Genesis 24:10–67

AIM

1. To tell the story of the quest for a bride for Isaac.
2. To help the children gain a clearer view of the background to the Bible stories.

INTRODUCTION

If they already know the story of Abraham merely refer to him and ask the name of the long-awaited son. Otherwise begin by talking about weddings and go on to point out that in other countries and other times things are done differently in some respects. Refer particularly to the custom of arranged marriages, and the care taken by parents to choose someone worthwhile and suitable for their children.

SUGGESTED PROCEDURE

Tell the story saying that now Abraham was old and Sarah had died, Abraham wanted to be sure that Isaac would have a wife to look after him.

1. A trustworthy servant is sent back to Mesopotamia for a bride. (Refer to the map.) Let the children put themselves in his shoes and feel his doubts, e.g. "What if she won't come back with me?" and the weight of responsibility he carried. Abraham, however, trusted in God.
2. The journey by camel. There was a retinue of servants and they brought gifts of silver, gold, clothes, etc.
3. Their arrival at the gate of the city in early evening. They knew that the women would soon be coming to draw water (as it was they who always did that chore). The servant prayed that the right girl would not only give him a drink when he asked but give his camels water also. What would that tell him about the kind of girl she was?
4. A very beautiful girl appeared carrying a pitcher on her shoulder.
5. The request for a drink and her response. Is this the right girl then?
6. The invitation to stay, and the warm welcome—with camels tended, the customary feet-washing and a meal. The servant, thankful to God for leading him, tells of his errand and finds the girl, Rebecca, and her family willing for the marriage to take place.
7. The journey home.
8. The meeting between Rebecca and Isaac, and their subsequent marriage. Abraham had trusted God to guide them and he had.

OPTIONAL ACTIVITIES

1. The chapter can be read with children taking the spoken parts and the teacher reading the narrative.
2. Discuss the character of the servant (dependable and trusting in God) and of Rebecca (kind and trusting).
3. Talk about the place of wells in village life. Draw pitchers, cut them out and make a frieze with them.

JACOB

INTRODUCTORY NOTE

It was from Isaac's son, Jacob (later given the name Israel), that the Jewish people are descended. In the story of Jacob we see God changing a weak, selfish character into a "prince with God". He and his twin brother Esau were different both in appearance and personality. Esau, the red-haired, outdoor-loving son was his father's favourite while Rebecca favoured the home-loving Jacob. The incident where Esau sold his birthright for a bowl of stew well illustrates the contrast between the brothers and at the same time highlights facets of Jacob's character that are apparent later in his story—the dogged determination to get what he wanted; the readiness to take advantage of circumstances, and to drive a hard bargain; the subtlety for which he is famous. The very name Jacob means usurper—as Esau bitterly pointed out when Jacob by deceit obtained the blessing which by custom went to the elder son. But there is something else. It would seem that Jacob wanted the birthright for himself—the rights and privileges of the firstborn, chief of which were that he became the spiritual leader of the family and was to be given a double share of the inheritance—because he had some perception of the value of spiritual things. He was struggling to understand what life was all about.

Like Abraham and Isaac he was one of the patriarchs, the founders of the Jewish faith, however inauspicious his beginning.

Lesson 1   Jacob and Esau

Genesis 25:21–34; 27

AIM

To tell the story of the quarrel between Jacob and Esau. To show that deceit and selfishness can bring unhappiness but that God is ready to help us to get rid of these.

INTRODUCTION

If the lessons on Abraham and Isaac have been done introduce Jacob and Esau as the children of Isaac and Rebecca. Alternatively, begin with a discussion asking children about the kind of people God helps. Do they have to be specially good? Is he only interested in holy people, ministers or priests, saints? Jacob was certainly none of these! This story is about someone who got to know God and gradually became a better person.

SUGGESTED PROCEDURE

The main points of the story are:

1. *Jacob Drives a Hard Bargain*
   Tell the story of Esau's selling of his birthright, explaining of course what this involved. Explore with the children (according to age and

ability) the moral aspects of the situation. Was it right for Jacob to strike such a bargain? After all, Esau didn't have to agree. Does the class approve of the action? If not, what do they think would have been the right thing to do? What does the incident tell us about Jacob? About Esau? Contrast the brothers' attitudes to the birthright. The smell of a good meal was too much for a hungry hunter. There were no instant foods in those days and food took a considerable time to prepare.

Isaac   Rebecca   Jacob   Esau

2. *Jacob Makes Sure of the Blessing* (Genesis 27)
   Either tell the story or read the chapter which is very dramatic. Having gained the birthright, Jacob's next step was to obtain by deception the blessing that properly belonged to the firstborn. It can be said in his favour that he valued it highly. Explain that Isaac was now old and, thinking that he was soon to die, was making his will and about to pass on to Esau the "blessing", i.e. the rights due to him. Probably the meal was part of the ritual of the occasion. Rebecca, overhearing his conversation with Esau, devised a plan to trick Isaac into giving the blessing to Jacob. Although his father's suspicions were aroused, Jacob managed to allay them and obtain the blessing, which may be found in Genesis 27:28–29.

3. *Esau's Anger* (Genesis 27:30–41)
   Esau returned and Jacob's deception was discovered. Verse 36 records his cry of frustration and fury. "This is the second time he has cheated me, no wonder he is called Jacob" (the Hebrew for "cheat" sounds like "Jacob"). Esau received a blessing but not *the* blessing. He hated Jacob and made up his mind that when Isaac had died (which he thought would be soon) he would kill his brother.

OPTIONAL ACTIVITIES

1. Discuss the moral implications of the story. With whom do the children's sympathies lie? All four people in the story have been hurt and made miserable—discuss each in turn. What do the children think should happen next?

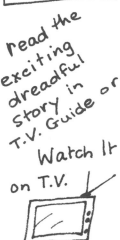

2. Ask the children to list the details of the blessing given to Jacob (Genesis 27:28–29). They could display it in ornate writing and decorate it.

Lesson 2 Jacob's Dream

Genesis 28:10–22

In the episode considered here we see Jacob guilty, lonely and miserable, and becoming aware that he is in the presence of God.

AIM

1. To tell the story of Jacob's dream.
2. To help the children to understand something of the awareness of God's presence.

INTRODUCTION

Briefly refer to the previous lesson, particularly Esau's threat to kill his brother.

Tell them that Rebecca heard of this threat and ask the children what they think will happen next.

SUGGESTED PROCEDURE

Tell the story emphasizing the following points:

1. *Leaving Home*

   His parents told Jacob that he had better make for his uncle's home in Haran many miles away. Reference to maps would be appropriate. Because of his dishonesty, he who loved being at home and who was his mother's favourite had to leave.

2. *The Dream*

   Describe his feelings—guilty, apprehensive, homesick and tired. Utterly lonely and feeling he was outwith God's care and protection, he lay down to sleep as best he could with stones for his pillow.

   Tell about the dream—a staircase with angels going up and down, and an assurance from God that he was not alone—"I am with you . . . I will not leave you", together with the promise of the land—the same promise as had been given to Abraham and Isaac.

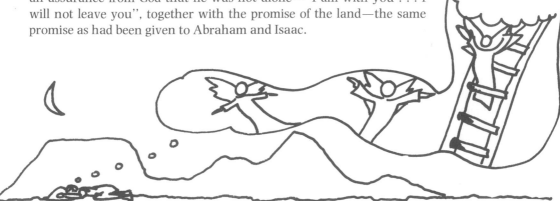

3. *Bethel*

   Next morning he awoke refreshed and reassured but at the same time feeling afraid. He knew God was there. "Surely the Lord is in this place and I did not know it. How awesome is this place!" He realized he would never forget that night and felt that he now knew God in a deeper way. He had heard of him before but had not felt God's closeness and interest in him. To mark the place as being holy he set up one of the stones he had used as a pillow and consecrated it. Bethel means "the house of God". He made a vow (Genesis 28:20–22).

   He went on his way with new courage, and eventually arrived at Laban's home. He married there and at long last came back to find Esau's rage had cooled. Isaac was still alive but there is no mention of Rebecca so it is assumed she had died. Jacob and his family of twelve sons and one daughter settled in the land God had promised to give to Abraham, Isaac and Jacob. God had been true to his promise, while Jacob was learning all the time to trust God more and more.

OPTIONAL ACTIVITIES

1. Sing: "God is always near me".
2. Read: Psalm 139:9–12 where the poet speaks of God's presence everywhere.

3. On dark paper draw a picture of Jacob, lonely under the stars, asleep. Remember it is a rocky place, and keep the sleeping figure small under the great bowl of the sky.
4. Do an abstract painting on the theme of fear and write a poem to go with it.
5. Discuss times when the children have felt that God was present. Perhaps in a cathedral, or looking at a sunset or perhaps in a much more personal setting. Such a discussion must be sensitively handled.

JOSEPH

INTRODUCTORY NOTE

Joseph, the favourite son of Jacob, rose to a position of great power in Egypt and through him the children of Israel eventually came to stay there. Though sold as a slave by his half-brothers and parted from his family for over twenty years he did not become embittered, recognizing that behind the actions of men there lay the purpose and kindness of God. The many fine traits in his character evidently sprang from his relationship with God.

AIM

To bring out the fact that God was over-ruling the events in Joseph's life and that, although it might seem like misery piled on misery, yet God was with him.

INTRODUCTION

The story of Joseph and his "coat of many colours" will probably be known to many of the children. Reference should be made to the family tree (page 21) to show Joseph's relationship to Abraham, Isaac and Jacob and it would be worth pointing out that the descendants promised to Abraham had now become quite numerous. In fact these twelve sons of Jacob were to become the founders of the twelve tribes that would form the nation of Israel.

The narrative in Genesis is easy to follow and if the children have Bibles they could read much of the story just as it stands. The story merits thoughtful discussion.

Groups in class take members of the family and write potted autobiographies.

Lesson 1   Joseph and His Brothers at Home in Canaan

Genesis 37:1–35

SUGGESTED PROCEDURE

Build up a picture of their semi-nomadic life. They were settled enough to grow crops but also had to move from time to time in search of fresh pastures for their sheep.

Joseph's coat was probably a sign that he was regarded by his father as the heir. It was a home that contained happiness and love on the one hand and hatred and misery on the other. Joseph may well have been spoiled and therefore become insensitive to others' feelings.

See *Start Here* for details about his childhood, dreams and arrival in Egypt. The following activities may be useful for recalling the main events.

OPTIONAL ACTIVITIES

1. Art: In dreams everyday things are often distorted and (as here) do strange things. Make a picture of the dreams. Try to suggest a dream-like quality, so that they look like dreams.
2. Discussion: The issue of jealousy is obvious here. Had the brothers reasons for their jealousy? For that degree of hatred? What were its consequences for Joseph, Jacob and the brothers themselves? What makes the children jealous? What can one do about feelings of jealousy?
3. Write a poem describing Joseph's feelings as he was taken off to an unknown land among strangers whose language he didn't understand—perhaps for ever.

Lesson 2   A Slave in Egypt

Genesis 39–41

AIM

To show how Joseph reacted to the test of being unjustly imprisoned for years.

INTRODUCTION

Build up a picture of ancient Egypt starting with what the children already know. Continue work on this as the story unfolds. Have pictures, maps, photographs, etc. Groups might investigate such topics as slavery, the Nile, clothing, food, transport, the army.

SUGGESTED PROCEDURE

Tell or read the story the stages of which are:

1. *Potiphar's House* (Genesis 39:1–6)
   Help the children to enter into Joseph's feelings as he stood un-comprehending in the market-place waiting to be bought just like an

animal or a piece of equipment. Describe his life in a wealthy Egyptian home and bring out the fact that, though he must have felt lonely as he thought of the home he was never to see again, yet he was not alone—"The Lord was with Joseph" (Verse 2). In time he became Potiphar's most trusted servant.

2. *Joseph in Prison* (Genesis 40; 41)
    Points to note:
    (a) After some time Potiphar was told a lie about Joseph and was so furious that he had him arrested and put in prison with his feet in chains and an iron collar round his neck. (Psalm 105:18 refers to this story.)
    (b) Potiphar had been pleased with him. Now the jailor was too and again he was given considerable responsibility. (The humiliation and responsibility would seem a good preparation for his future position of authority.)
    (c) Dreams again—and their fulfilment. Joseph's hopes were raised but were doomed to disappointment as he was forced to the conclusion that the wine steward had forgotton all about him. It looked as if God had forgotten him too but see Genesis 39:21.
    (d) Two years later, more dreams (Genesis 41) and their interpretation with Joseph's plan for dealing with the imminent plenty and famine.
    (e) Joseph was appointed Governor of Egypt—the equivalent of Prime Minister.

Egyptian jailer

crimes punished by beating torture or execution

OPTIONAL ACTIVITIES

1. Discussion: Joseph had experienced one apparent misfortune after another. Get the children to list them. He was tested in prison. How? What was he being tested for? How did he stand up to the test? What was it that kept him going? What do his various experiences show us of the character of Joseph? Discuss these and similar questions (perhaps duplicated) in small groups for about four minutes and report back to the class.
2. Art:
    (a) Potiphar was captain of Pharaoh's guard. One group could find out about the Egyptian army and make drawings and weapons.

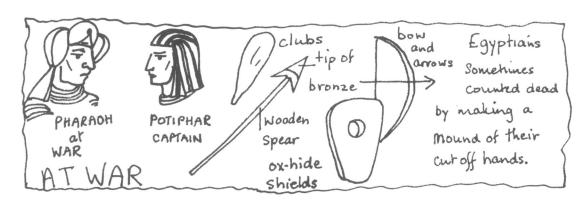

PHARAOH at WAR

POTIPHAR CAPTAIN

AT WAR

clubs
tip of bronze
wooden spear
ox-hide shields

bow and arrows

Egyptians sometimes counted dead by making a mound of their cut off hands.

(b) Another group could investigate food —beginning with the baker and wine steward!

(c) Joseph as Prime Minister met many well-dressed people. One group could find out about clothes. Each child could make a ceremonial collar of thin cardboard and decorate it with foil, pasta shapes, buttons, etc.

(d) Some children might like to paint the dreams in this section. Remember they were dreams so things need not be lifelike, just recognizable—that should encourage some.

3. Maths: Let the children calculate how long Joseph was in Egypt by the time he became Prime Minister. (Genesis 37:2 and Genesis 41:46—13 years.)

Lesson 3   Joseph Reunited with His Brothers

Genesis 42 -46; 47: 1–12

AIM

To tell the story of how the Israelites came to settle in Egypt. To show that God was active throughout, carrying out his purpose.

INTRODUCTION

Refer to Joseph's exalted circumstances in Egypt—an important position, a wife, two sons and a big house. How often must he have remembered his family back in Canaan! Ask such questions as: What would his thoughts have been when remembering his father? Benjamin? His older brothers? Perhaps some children will think of revenge. This could lead to a useful discussion on the subject of getting one's own back. Tell them that the time was coming when Joseph would have the opportunity to have his revenge.

SUGGESTED PROCEDURE

Tell the story or read it. Some points for consideration might be:

1. (Genesis 42:6). The brothers entered bowing low. What does this remind the children of? How was it that he recognized them but they did not recognize him? What thoughts might he have had? (Is my father alive? Are my brothers still as cruel and deceitful as ever?) He wanted to find the answers to such questions and the only way was to test the brothers. This is the reason for the money in the sacks, etc. It is important that the children understand this.

2. Explain what is meant by speaking through an interpreter (Genesis 42:23).

3. The plot is rather complex. For clarity the action will be summarized in the column with comments and suggestions alongside.

(a) *Brothers' First Visit*

Imprisoned for three days	Presumably to impress on them that he meant what he said.
Kept Simeon Others went home for the youngest brother. Money in their sacks.	How did it get there? Why?

Egyptian Necklace

Collect, dry, paint and string melon seeds, macaroni make your own!

$| = 1$

$\cap = 10$

$\mathcal{C} = 100$

$\check{\bar{\zeta}} = 1\,000$

$\theta = 10\,000$

$= 100\,000$

$= 1\,000\,000$

$13 = \cap |||$

$42 = \cap\cap\cap\cap ||$

$405 = \mathcal{CCCC}$
$\qquad |||||$

(b) *Back in Canaan*
Second visit proposed
Reuben and Judah pledged
themselves to bring
Benjamin back.

(c) *Second Visit*
Brought gifts, twice as much
money and Benjamin with
them.

Joseph entertained them.	Why were they amazed at the seating arrangements?
They return home but are overtaken—cup in Benjamin's sack.	
All went back to Joseph who said he would keep Benjamin while the rest went free.	Why did he say this?
Judah offered to take Benjamin's place.	What did the test show about the brothers?
Joseph told them who he was.	What was the effect on the brothers? Why? (See Genesis 44:16) What guilt? Revenge or mercy—which is better?

Joseph reassured his brothers that all was forgiven and sent for his
father. They all came to settle in Egypt.

Joseph's verdict on the whole story is the key to his character, "It was
really God who sent me . . ."

OPTIONAL ACTIVITIES

1. Read: Psalm 105:1–23.

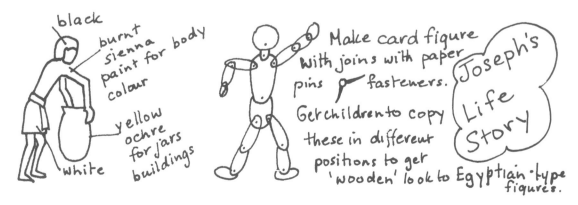

2. Art: Make a frieze showing the main events in Joseph's life. Do it in the
Egyptian style where faces are shown in profile but the shoulders and
body full on.

3. Plan an interview with Joseph after the final event.

MOSES

INTRODUCTORY NOTE

Moses, son of Hebrew slaves, is one of the great figures of history. Adopted by an Egyptian princess and educated in all the wisdom of the Egyptians, it was he who led the Israelites out of Egypt and through the Sinai desert where they were forged into a nation. Though he led them to the border of the land promised so many years before to Abraham, Moses himself did not enter it.

The Exodus (a going out) is the key event in the history of Old Testament Israel. The journey from Egypt to Canaan is, in a sense, a historical parable in which God, by the actions he took, was showing the kind of God he is. Following generations were then pointed back to the written record as a revelation of what God is like—a God who acts. The escape from Egypt was (and still is) celebrated in the annual festival of the Passover which became a means of instructing the children. The Exodus probably took place in the early 13th century B.C. about the time of Rameses II.

Family Tree of Abraham

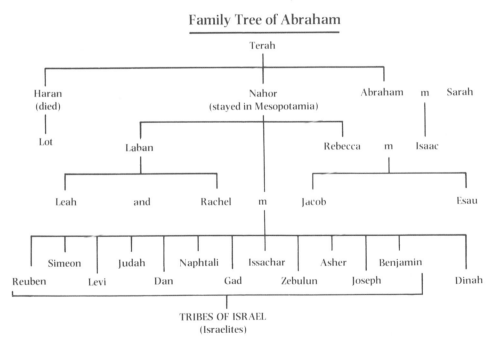

TRIBES OF ISRAEL
(Israelites)

Lesson 1   Moses in Egypt

Exodus 1 and 2

AIM

To build up a picture of life in ancient Egypt. To show the oppression under which the Israelites lived. To make clear the choice Moses had to make.

INTRODUCTION

If the children know the story of Joseph remind them that Jacob and his family went to live in Egypt and their many descendants still lived there four hundred years later. They were no longer a free people honoured and respected but were slaves, despised and feared.

The children could do some research on ancient Egypt to help put the events of Moses' life in their geographical and historical setting and to make clear the choice Moses made when he decided to identify himself with the Israelite slaves rather than with the royal family. Relevant aspects might be:

(a) Egypt's dependence on the Nile (6690 km) for fishing, transport and irrigation.

(b) Mapwork showing the Nile delta, lower and upper Egypt, Thebes, Rameses, Sukkoth, the Red Sea and Sinai.

(c) Large building projects undertaken by the Pharaohs with the help of slave labour. Explain how bricks were shaped from mud and straw and left to dry in the hot sun. The Sphinx and the pyramids were already old at the time of Moses.

(d) The religion of ancient Egypt. Mention might be made of the Nile-god and Ra the sun-god.

(e) Egyptian writing.

(f) Education.

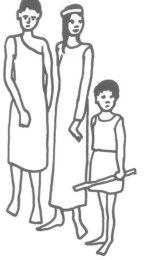

Hebrew Family

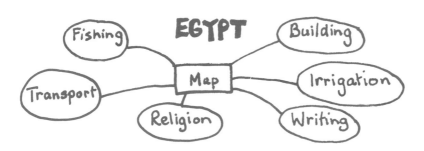

SUGGESTED PROCEDURE

Bring out the choice that lay before Moses:

1. Tell of the splendours of Egypt from the point of view of one of the princesses and her adopted son. From the class's research deduce the kind of upbringing and education he would have had and emphasize the prospects before him. Some children might know his name if they know the story of baby Moses.

2. Read: Exodus 1:1–14 or have it duplicated. Ask questions such as:
   (a) Why was the king of Egypt afraid of the Israelites?
   (b) In what ways did he make their lives miserable?

3. Moses' choice (Genesis 2:11–16). Have the children list the factors that might have weighed with him as he had to decide whether to identify with the palace or his own people. Remind them that he had been nursed by his mother and presumably was in touch with his brother Aaron and sister Miriam (both older than he). He chose to suffer with God's people.

Egyptians

OPTIONAL ACTIVITIES

1. Project work connected with Egypt, e.g. paintings or models of pyramids, chariots, treasures, etc.

2. In contrast a picture of Israelite slaves at work should be made. Children could choose some words from Hebrews 11:24, for a caption.
3. Make mud bricks. Pour a mixture of earth, water and clay into a mould (an empty tea packet would do) and when dry remove the mould. Try another one adding straw or grass to the mixture, and find out which is stronger.
4. Difficult choices face everyone at one time or another. Discuss Moses' choice. Was it the right one? Talk about choices the children have had to make. Some might like to write about a time when they had to make a big choice or a difficult one—not always the same thing!

Lesson 2   Moses Confronts Pharaoh

Exodus 3; 4:10–16; 5; 7–10; 12:1–13

AIM

1. To show how the Israelites escaped from Egypt.
2. To show that God helped Moses to do things that he had thought would be too difficult for him.

INTRODUCTION

Refer to the misery of the slaves in Egypt. Ask the children what they could do about it. Read Exodus 2:23–25. The covenant was God's promise to make them into a nation and to give them a land. God was about to do just that.

SUGGESTED PROCEDURE

The main points of the story to bring out are:

1. *A Leader Is Needed*
   Ask the children, "What sort of man would you choose to lead the people out of Egypt?"

2. *God's Choice of a Leader*

Using Bibles (or duplicated passages) and dictionaries have the children discuss in small groups the following verses and questions:

Exodus 3:1–10, 11–13, 15.

Exodus 4:10–16.

What sort of man was Moses?

Was he ambitious? bold? confident? curious? determined? different? headstrong? reluctant?

How does he compare with the leader described in 1. above?

3. *Bricks Without Straw*

Now he had to face Pharaoh. Read Exodus 5 and let the children dramatize it.

Point out that things had become worse, not better, as a result of the interview. Discuss how Moses would be feeling.

4. *The Nine Plagues*

One way of looking at them is to regard the matter as a contest between the gods of Egypt and the God of Moses. The sequence of events follows a logical order and probably lasted about a year.

(a) The Nile turns to blood (Exodus 7:14–24).

(b) Frogs, driven from the river banks, make for the houses (Exodus 8:1–15).

(c) Gnats (Exodus 8:16–19).

(d) Flies (Exodus 8:20–32).

(e) Disease of the animals (Exodus 9:1–7).

(f) Skin infections on people (Exodus 9:8–12).

(g) Hail (Exodus 9:12–35).

(h) Locusts (Exodus 10:1–20).

(i) Darkness (Exodus 10:21–29).

5. *The First Passover*

If the children have Bibles let them read Exodus 12:1–13 and then fill in the blanks in this previously duplicated passage. Alternatively, duplicate the Bible passage also.

"On the .... day of this month let each man take a .... or a .... for his family. On the .... day of the month, in the ...., let all the Israelites kill the victim. Mark the doorposts with some of the .... the meat and eat it quickly with .... and .... Be dressed for travel with your .... on your feet and with your .... in your hand. On that night I shall pass through the land of Egypt and .... every firstborn of man and beast. When I see the .... on the doorway, I will .... you.

Mobile using
Nylon thread
card
feltpens
cane

OPTIONAL ACTIVITIES

1. Make a frieze on the theme of the plagues.

2. Discuss:
   (a) What makes the children afraid? How do they overcome their fears?
   (b) The difficulties of standing up for what is right when others are against you.

Lesson 3   The Pursuit

Exodus 13:21–22; 14:5–31; 15:1–21

AIM

To show how the Israelites learned that God could be trusted to keep them safe?

INTRODUCTION

Use a map to show the route taken by the Israelites and the point they had reached in their flight. Show how the pursuing Egyptians were in a very strong position, having driven the Israelites to the Red Sea. There seemed no possible escape for them. Explain too, that God had led them using a cloud by day and fire by night.

SUGGESTED PROCEDURE

Tell the story as dramatically as you can, making the following points:
   1. Pharaoh changes his mind about letting them go.
   2. The Israelites panic.
   3. Moses prays.
   4. God gives Moses his instructions.
   5. The pillar of cloud moves to a new position, behind the Israelites.

25

6. Moses obeys God's instructions and the way through the Red Sea opens. A strong east wind holds the waters back.
7. The Israelites cross.
8. The Egyptians follow.
9. The waters return.
10. The Israelites see God's power and trust him.
11. Moses sings a song of victory. (See Exodus 25.)

OPTIONAL ACTIVITIES

Language:

(a) Write an account of these events as seen through the eyes of a child who had to help an aged grandparent along.

(b) Make up a song of praise to a tune you know or compose a tune to go with it. Some children could add Miriam's dance while the song was being sung.

(c) Have the children read on to tape, play-wise, Exodus 14:5–31, and some of Exodus 15 with sound effects and a musical accompaniment to add to the atmosphere.

Lesson 4   In the Wilderness

Exodus 20

AIM

To teach that God has rules that have to be obeyed.

INTRODUCTION

The Israelites soon began to complain. Exodus 16 gives examples of how God provided food for the large company. His method of dealing with them was designed to teach them obedience and reliance upon him. The Ten Commandments set out the basic ethical standards God requires of all. Discuss the need for rules. Are they necessary? Suppose there were no class rules, school rules, etc. Do the children have rules at home? Point out that there are lots of rules we obey though we're scarcely aware of them. The bigger the group, the more the rules—is that true? Spend some time on this topic.

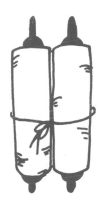

SUGGESTED PROCEDURE

1. Discuss the necessity for the Israelites having rules—to govern relationships among themselves. But that was not all. God expected a certain standard from them. They were his people.
2. Tell how God called Moses to meet with him on Mount Sinai to receive his rules for his people.
3. Make a scroll of the Ten Commandments and unroll it as each is read and commented on. It is necessary to think each one through and to make clear its relevance to the present day. The first four relate to man-towards-God attitudes and conduct while the remaining six are concerned with relationships between people.

OPTIONAL ACTIVITIES

1. Learn the Ten Commandments.
2. Make a decorative panel incorporating the Ten Commandments.

3. Add Jesus' summary of the Commandments to the panel (Luke 10:27).
4. This might be a good time to do a lesson on the Passover so one follows. Alternatively, the whole module could begin with it and the rest of the story be told as an explanation of its origin—or the lesson may be omitted altogether.

Lesson 5   The Passover

Exodus 12:21–28
Deuteronomy 16:1–8

AIM

To give the children an understanding of a festival that is still important to Jewish people today.

INTRODUCTION

Have pictures of a Jewish family celebrating this meal which follows a fairly standard form.

SUGGESTED PROCEDURE

1. Describe the meal with the use of drawings or substitutes. There would be four cups of wine, herbs, salt water, three flat cakes of unleavened bread, roast lamb.

The ritual has these elements in it:
(a) The opening prayer then the first cup of wine is passed round.
(b) Each person takes herbs and dips them in salt water.
(c) The father breaks one of the cakes of bread and puts it aside.
(d) The youngest child asks, "What do these things mean?"
(e) The father tells the story of the first Passover and Psalms 113 and 114 are sung.
(f) The second cup is passed round.
(g) All wash their hands, grace is said and bread is broken before the meal proper starts.
(h) Bitter herbs dipped in sauce are distributed.
(i) The meal of roast lamb is taken.
(j) The third cup and bread are passed round.
(k) Psalms 115–118 and 136 are sung.
(l) The final cup of wine is passed round.
2. Ask if the children can suggest what the various elements symbolize.
3. Tell them that Jewish families celebrate the Passover every year.

Lesson 6   The Promised Land in Sight

Numbers 13:17–20
Deuteronomy 1:19–33

AIM

To tell about the Israelites lack of faith despite all that God had done for them.

INTRODUCTION

Discuss what the children think Moses would want to know about the promised land. Make a list. Now make a list of what he did want to know (Numbers 13:17–20) and compare the two.

SUGGESTED PROCEDURE

Tell the story of the spies:
(a) Moses chooses twelve and gives them their instructions.
(b) They return, ten report and the people react.
(c) Caleb and Joshua report and the people react.
(d) The result was that they did not enter the land then but spent almost forty years in the wilderness. In Deuteronomy we have a series of addresses given by Moses to the people as they were finally about to enter Canaan and in Deuteronomy 1:6–8 and 19–33 he recalls this event.

Fix roll of paper into Box

On the paper you have fixed the children's pictures

OPTIONAL ACTIVITIES

1. Drama: Mime the story with suitable background music. Express the different emotions—the fear of the people, the frustration of Joshua and Caleb, etc.
2. Language:
   (a) Be reporters (television, radio or newspaper) interviewing the spies on their return.
   (b) "We even saw giants!"
   "We felt like grasshoppers."
   "They live in cities with walls that reach the sky."
   Make up more exaggerations. Weave them into a story. Talk about the effect exaggeration can have.
   (c) Write a poem about the Land of Promise. Begin "Is it a land where . . ."
   (d) With mature children discuss the fact that the minority was right.
3. Craft: Make a large bunch of grapes for use in drama.

Tape the programme of Canaan News and play as you turn the 'T.V.'

Lesson 7   Death of Moses

Deuteronomy 6:20 –25; 8:6–16; 31:7–8; 34

INTRODUCTION

Tell how after 40 years God told Moses he would not enter the land himself but would see it.

SUGGESTED PROCEDURE

Read some of Moses' addresses to the people. Joshua was to be Moses' successor. Read Deuteronomy 34.

OPTIONAL ACTIVITIES

1. Language: Write a short biography of Moses, not more than 150 words. (The teacher may wish to refer to a similar résumé of Moses' life in Hebrews 11:23–28.)
2. Psalms: Several psalms recount the story of the Exodus, e.g. 77, 78, 105, 106, 114, 136. Some children might like to try a long narrative poem or ballad themselves before reading some of these psalms.

JOSHUA AND THE CAPTURE OF JERICHO

Lesson 1   Spying out the Land

Joshua 1 and 2

AIM

To tell the story of Rahab who helped to carry out God's plan by hiding the spies and to show that she was saved because of her faith in God.

INTRODUCTION

Set the scene using these background notes. After the death of Moses God chose Joshua to lead the Israelites into the promised land. The Israelites were on the east of the River Jordan with the mountains of Moab behind them, while those of the district of Jericho were on the west. The rocky walls of the mountains shut them in and the valley of the Jordan lay between. The Jordan, a winding river which at that time was in spate, lay between them and the strong, walled city of Jericho.

White cartridge paper soaked in weak tea and edges torn make effective 'antique' map.

SUGGESTED PROCEDURE

1. Discuss what a good leader would do before attacking. Describe how spies would be chosen for courage, daring and initiative. Picture them swimming across the Jordan—hiding till dark in a forest perhaps and eventually going through the gates of Jericho. (This could lead to imaginative discussion and suggestions.)

Ancient Jericho
In broad plain in Jordan Valley 840' below sea level
Oldest inhabited city of Man . . . excavated in centre of modern Jericho

Walls of Double Card – pour polyfilla in between layers or

Build Houses of Shoe Boxes and join up with card

papier mâché hills

MODEL

A Fortress City Thick walls Houses in the walls

2. Describe the city walls, broad enough for houses to be built on top.
3. Rahab's house would be the first they came to. Tell how safe she and all the people might feel as they looked down into the valley below at the River Jordan with the mountains beyond. A simple map could be used.

4. Discuss the feelings of the people when they heard that an enemy had gathered on the opposite bank of the river, waiting to attack. Imagine the talk in Jericho and the stories they may have heard about previous victories by those Israelites who said that God was on their side.

5. Discuss how they would begin to prepare for battle—laying in food, water, wood, etc.

6. Explain that although Rahab does not understand, she believes God will keep his promise—that he will give Jericho into the hands of the Israelites. She decides to be on their side and trust in their God.

7. Tell the story dramatically from Joshua 2:2–22. Men seen as they entered; arrival reported to the king. Rahab hides them on the flat roof under stalks of flax drying there. She deceives the soldiers sent out to look for them. After the soldiers have gone outside the city to find the spies, Rahab reveals that she believes in their God, and arranges to help the men escape out of a window by a scarlet rope. She tells them to hide in the hills for three days until the hue and cry has died down. Picture Rahab pleading for her life and for the safety of her family when they come to attack. She is given a promise that if she hangs the scarlet rope out of her window her household will be spared. The spies recross the river and tell Joshua all that has happened.

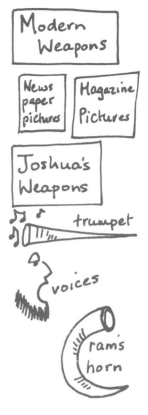

OPTIONAL ACTIVITIES

1. Children could pretend to be inhabitants of Jericho; groups could gather together talking about what is going on as the city prepares for battle.

ESCAPE FROM CITY

2. Make a frieze of the city surrounded by the strong walls, with houses on top, including Rahab's; spies climbing down the scarlet rope; men creeping away towards the hills.

3. The story could be used as a basis for a discussion about walled cities in Bible times and generally; also types of houses in these days may be discussed. A number of teachers' books and pupils' books discuss life in the lands of the Bible.

Lesson 2   The Fall of Jericho

Joshua 6

AIM

To tell how Jericho was captured through the obedience of Joshua to God.

INTRODUCTION

By questioning, establish the main points of the previous lesson. Emphasize:

(a) Jericho was the way into the promised land.

(b) Joshua was commanded to cross the River Jordan and take Jericho.

SUGGESTED PROCEDURE

1. Describe the shock, bewilderment and fear as people of Jericho one day find the Israelites across the river, outside the walls of their city. Only one person was glad and excited!

2. Outline the method of attack. For six days they would march round the city in silence, once every day, armed guard in front, seven priests blowing trumpets, and the priests carrying the covenant box, followed by the rest of the people. (For background on the covenant box see Exodus 25:10–22.)

3. Describe vividly the feelings of the people in the city of Jericho, as the same strange activity happened every day. Would they laugh? No. They seemed to be terrified by the silent people, the steady tramp of feet and the blowing of trumpets. They wondered what would happen next.

4. On the seventh day the Israelites marched round seven times. Trumpets sounded, people shouted loudly, the walls fell down and the city was taken.

5. Rahab and all her family were brought safely out of their house. How did the soldiers know which one was hers? (The scarlet rope hangs out of the window.) Because they trusted in God, they were taken to safety to the camp of the Israelites. Picture their joy and how they would have thanked God for the marvellous things he had done for them.

OPTIONAL ACTIVITIES

1. Art: Add to the frieze figures marching round the city.

2. Sing: "Joshua fought the battle of Jericho" or "Round the Walls of Jericho".

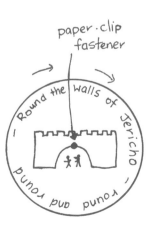

Large circle card
small card cut out shape
of city with gate
Draw soldiers on   Fix together with fastener.

GIDEON

Lesson 1   An Unusual Leader

Judges 6:2–24, 36–40

AIM

To show that God may use unexpected people to do important tasks.

INTRODUCTION

The Midianites were nomads who lived in the region east and south-east of the Dead Sea. From time to time they raided the land of Palestine and settled temporarily there. The Israelites were often forced to retreat to caves in the mountains.

SUGGESTED PROCEDURE

1. Introduce Gideon the son of Joash, a farmer. Discuss what type of work he would do to help his father on the farm: caring for sheep, ploughing, harvesting, working in a vineyard, and compare perhaps with farming today.

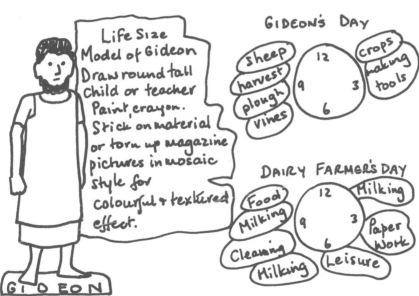

2. Describe a day at harvest time. One day Gideon is admiring a field of ripe wheat when he becomes aware of a cloud of dust on the horizon—realizes it is a horde of Midianites riding on camels—his family run into hiding and watch in horror while the army devastate their crop. Gideon thinks God has forsaken them.
3. But Gideon was wrong. God had heard the prayers of the Israelites and was going to provide a leader who would help them to drive out their enemies.

4. What qualities would be necessary in such a leader. Would a farmer like Gideon be suitable?
5. Describe the incidents in the winepress and with the fleeces where God's messenger appeared to him and proved to his surprise that he was the leader whom God had chosen. Emphasize: (1) Meal set on fire; (2) The tests of the fleece; (3) God's encouragement.

OPTIONAL ACTIVITIES
1. Ask the children to draw Gideon working on the farm.
2. Act out the story showing how the Israelites felt during the raid.

Lesson 2 An Unusual Test

Judges 7:1–8

AIM
To show that God does not need great numbers to carry out his plans.

INTRODUCTION
Write on blackboard the summary shown below.

Number of volunteers	32 000
Number who went home because they were afraid	22 000
Number left	10 000
Number who failed test	9 700
Number in army	300

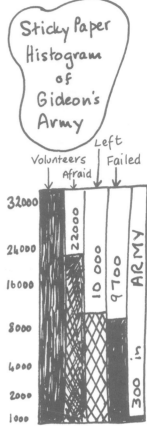

SUGGESTED PROCEDURE
1. Go over the main points of the previous lesson and explain that God told Gideon to use an army to fight the Midianites.
2. Refer to the above blackboard summary and explain that Gideon had too many volunteers because God wanted men who would rely on him rather than on their own strength and ability. Discuss different reasons for their volunteering to fight, e.g. revenge, adventure, etc.
3. Ask the children what kind of test they might have expected Gideon to give the ten thousand who were not afraid.
4. Describe the unusual test. With God's help Gideon chose the right men. Discuss why these men were selected. Was it that those who lapped the water from their hands would always be prepared for sudden attack?

OPTIONAL ACTIVITIES
1. Discuss different types of tests which the children may have experienced, e.g. test to gain a Brownie badge, swimming, etc.
2. Challenge the children to devise an up-to-date method of selecting ten brave men out of a hundred volunteers for some specific purpose (e.g. a search and rescue operation).

3. Ask the children to pretend that they are one of the rejected volunteers, writing home to their family. How would they explain why they had not been chosen?

Lesson 3   An Unusual Battle

Judges 7:9–21

AIM

To show how God gave victory to those who trusted him.

INTRODUCTION

Refer to the previous lesson.

SUGGESTED PROCEDURE

1. The Israelites now had a leader and an army—but how did the leader feel? Gideon was afraid, but read how God encouraged him in verses 9–15.
2. Were they now ready to go into battle? What about a plan of attack and weapons? Ask the children to suggest weapons that they would expect Gideon's men to have. Read the relevant passage (verses 16–21) to the class and build up together the plan of attack, summarizing it on the blackboard. Ask the children what the men were to carry, then draw on the board, a trumpet, a jar and a torch.
3. Describe the scene with the Midianites encamped in the valley—an enormous show of strength compared with Gideon's three hundred men! Go on to describe the confusion and panic of the battle when the Midianites saw the lights and heard the sound of the trumpets and the war cry "A sword for the Lord and for Gideon". So Gideon's army had not needed conventional weapons after all. Following God's plan, they had been successful in driving out their enemies, and the Israelites lived in peace for the rest of Gideon's life.

OPTIONAL ACTIVITIES

1. Make a frieze of the battle scene.
2. Write an eye-witness account of the battle.

Trust in God

illustrated texts for Bookmarks

Play: SWORD DRILL

- SHEATH SWORDS (Bibles under arms)
- DRAW SWORDS (Hold up Bibles)
- CALL out verse of Bible
- CHARGE (Look up verse)

Papier Mâché Model of Area
Use flags to represent armies

RUTH

Ruth 1–4

INTRODUCTORY NOTE

The story of Ruth is a quiet one set among more violent scenes of the Judges period of Jewish history. To appreciate it fully one has to understand the following customs of the time:

(a) When widowed, even early in life, a woman could be regarded as "a servant of the dead man's family".

(b) Her husband's nearest relative was expected by Hebrew law to assume responsibility for her, even to marry her. (Ruth's appeal in Chapter 3 may sound strange to our ears but was in accordance with customs of the day!)

(c) Gleaning was a Hebrew custom (one of Moses' agricultural laws) of allowing the poor to gather what was left of grain or grapes when reapers had done their work.

(d) To settle a business deal, a sandal was often passed from the seller to the buyer of any property. (See Ruth 4:7.)

AIM

To show how loyalty and a sense of her responsibility when faced with an easier option led Ruth to a fuller and more interesting life.

INTRODUCTION

In preceding days, whether in creative writing or discussion, focus the children's thinking on ideas of loyalty. Animals will figure largely at first (e.g. Emma, Radar, etc.); lead from these to their own experiences and extend questioning to imaginary situations where each child has to decide what he/she would do, given certain circumstances. If possible, develop their thinking to consider older people in our society—this has to be done sensitively but children nearly always respond well (and very idealistically!) to this challenge.

SUGGESTED PROCEDURE

It is a good story to narrate in one telling. How much detail is given or moral drawn depends largely on the individual teacher and class. Most children enjoy the first; the second may be built into the narration around the fact of Ruth's loyalty to Naomi and her refusal of the offer of greater freedom (and more fun!) to follow what was then regarded to be her duty.

The story falls naturally into five parts and for dramatic purposes it is advisable to have the following salient facts at one's "fingertips".

1. (Chapter 1) During famine in Israel, Naomi and Elimelech take their two sons to Moab. There they marry local girls, Orpah and Ruth, but quite soon all three men die. Naomi, homesick and hearing of good harvests back home, decides to return there. Orpah stays but Ruth goes back with Naomi; make much of the scenes depicted in verses 6–18, entering into the emotions that would be felt by each of the three

people. Describe the arrival in Bethlehem at the start of the barley harvest.

2. (Chapter 2) Introduce Boaz, a wealthy relative of Elimelech. Ruth "gleans" in his fields, becomes known to him and begins to receive favours (verses 13–16). Naomi hears this and recognizes God's hand in it all: "The Lord always keeps his promises" (verse 20).

3. (Chapter 3) Naomi wants Ruth to be married again and makes plans (to us, very strange ones!), see verses 1–5. Ruth thus finds opportunity to appeal to Boaz's sense of family responsbility. He, however, remembers a still closer relative whose responsibility it might be, gives her nevertheless a generous gift of barley and sends her off home before anyone finds her (verses 14–15). Naomi advises patience!

4. (Chapter 4, verses 1–10) The nearer relative, in the presence of a town council, turns down the chance to purchase one of Elimelech's fields when he hears that Ruth is included in the bargain. Here we see the symbolic act of the exchange of a sandal (verses 1–8). Boaz is now the owner of all the property and marries Ruth (verses 9–10).

5. (Chapter 4, verses 13–22) The birth of a son, Obed, the grandfather of King David . . . and an ancestor of Jesus himself.

Barley

OPTIONAL ACTIVITIES

1. Make a collage of:
   (a) Orpah waving goodbye to Naomi and Ruth.
   (b) A gleaning scene.
   (c) The exchange of a sandal (under the shade of a tree, perhaps?) at the town council.
   (d) Boaz and Ruth together at the end of the story.

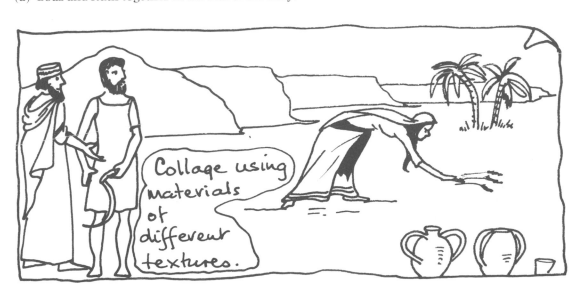

Collage using materials of different textures.

2. Some children may enjoy composing a ballad (set to a familiar tune) retelling the story.

3. Find out more about customs and symbols of other times or other countries. Discuss these and compare with those of today.

THE STORY OF DAVID

Lesson 1   David at King Saul's Court

1 Samuel 17:55 to 18: 16; 19:1–9; 20:1–42

AIM

To tell a story of loyalty and courage in difficult circumstances.

INTRODUCTION

Refer briefly to the story of David and Goliath (see *Start Here*).

SUGGESTED PROCEDURE

1. Tell how David's life is changed for ever after his defeat of Goliath. Saul commands David to remain in his service, playing the harp at court when Saul is depressed, and fighting in the army where he proves to be a successful officer. The famous friendship grows between David and Saul's son Jonathan. It is when David becomes popular with the people that Saul's jealousy is aroused and, with his mental instability, the situation begins to look dangerous for David.

2. Conflict arises not only between the jealous king and David but also between Jonathan's loyalty to his father and to his great friend. Role-play of the interview between Saul and Jonathan would emphasize how much Jonathan was prepared to do to help David. An absolute monarch, of uncertain temper, had to be approached carefully. Another aspect is David's loyalty to Saul, in spite of the attacks upon him, for he continues to serve in Saul's army.

Shepherd boy

Soldier

Musician

Accused

King

Samuel

King Saul

David

3. Jonathan attempts to restore relationships between David and Saul. By this time David is aware that there is real danger for him in appearing at court and so plans are made. A tape of the conversation in 1 Samuel 20:1–23, with possibly a little editing, would make the situation come alive and arouse discussion about their friendship with its loyalties. Children might speculate on the possible outcome. A second tape, a reading or story-telling of the events that follow should give an exciting climax. David leaves Saul's court for ever.

OPTIONAL ACTIVITIES

1. Artwork could include scenes at court, and in the fields.

2. Discussions could arise on loyalties, friendships, standards of behaviour, and how these affect others.
3. The tape conversations suggested above could be developed further.

Lesson 2   David the Outlaw Who Became King

1 Samuel 22:1–2; 23:19–29; 24:1–22; 26:1–25
1 Chronicles 10

AIM

To show how David returned good for evil.

INTRODUCTION

Ask the children how they feel and behave when they have been treated unfairly or blamed for something that they have not done.

SUGGESTED PROCEDURE

1. David is now a hunted man on the run. As might be expected, men gather to follow him—men with many different attitudes and motives, yet under David's leadership they become an orderly and disciplined band.

How would I feel if wrongly accused?

stories

from

David's

Life

Photos of David

2. Escaping from Saul, David flees into the hills, to wooded country, some three miles south of Hebron. Here he has his last meeting with Jonathan who again encourages him. The account of David's whereabouts being made known to Saul, and of Saul's forces pursuing David and his men, make a dramatic story. David and his men are being surrounded and their enemies are closing in. Word comes to Saul of a Philistine attack and the whole operation is called off in the nick of time. God had protected his servant.

3. David is hiding in the caves (by the shores of the Dead Sea about halfway along the western side) when Saul himself comes in and is thus at David's mercy. In spite of his men's urgings, David has too great a regard for Saul to have his revenge. When he calls to Saul he pleads his innocence of any intention to harm or kill him and Saul's heart is softened—for the time being.

4. David and a companion deliberately set out to pick their way through the Israelite camp as the army sleeps, right up to the spot where Saul is lying. Again Saul is at his mercy and David is urged to kill him, but declares that he will not touch the anointed king. He calls to Saul, pleading for him to believe in his continued loyalty. Saul is filled with remorse—but only for a while!

5. In a great battle at Mount Gilboa, south-west of Lake Galilee, the Philistines defeat Israel and Saul and Jonathan are killed. David is acclaimed king in Judah and later throughout Israel.

OPTIONAL ACTIVITIES

1. Discuss the influence of others on our behaviour, e.g. the temptation to follow the crowd. Talk about David's refusal to harm Saul, and how we should respect those in authority.
2. Art: Illustrate David's adventures.
3. Prayer: Lord, help us to think before we act
   and to do what we know to be right.

ELIJAH, THE FIERY PROPHET

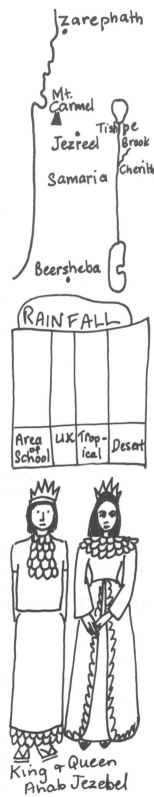

Zarephath

Mt. Carmel

Jezreel

Tishbe

Brook Cherith

Samaria

Beersheba

RAINFALL

Area of School	UK	Trop- ical	Desert

King & Queen
Ahab Jezebel

INTRODUCTORY NOTE

Elijah lived about eight to nine hundred years before Christ—about 2800 years ago. He was a prophet, i.e. a spokesman for God, at a time when the people of Israel were forgetting their previous teaching and adopting many of the heathen practices of the nations round about. It can be explained to the children that God had to pick out certain people through whom to speak. These were usually men who followed his ways closely and to whom he often gave miraculous powers as well as words of wisdom (only sometimes about the future).

Ahab and Jezebel were king and queen for a large part of Elijah's life. They were wicked people who did some very cruel things and encouraged their subjects to worship Baal—one of the Baalim of surrounding nations. These were "gods of the land, owning and controlling it. The increase of crops, fruit and cattle was under their control". It was against this that Elijah had to fight.

Lesson 1   Elijah and the Drought

1 Kings 17

AIM

To show through the story of this prophet that God can give strength and provision in unlikely circumstances; to show also that that same care can be shown by one person to another.

INTRODUCTION

Choose an everyday incident (topical if possible) where a "representative" has had to come to school, e.g. school trip planned, organizer from the Travel Agency becomes ill on the day of the parents' meeting and his representative has to come instead. Discuss what sort of person this should be:

someone who knows the plan;

someone who can put the story over clearly;

someone who knows where to find all the necessary answers.

Have the children ever had to represent anyone anywhere? What responsibilities did they have?

SUGGESTED PROCEDURE

1. Elijah knew God in a special way. As he had been growing up, he had seen around him the worship of Baal with its claim that it was he who sent the rain and caused the crops to grow, etc. Elijah also saw the cruelty that went along with it—sometimes even human sacrifices!

But surely his own living God was the Provider? In verse1, he decides to prove this to King Ahab who was leading the Israelites astray. "There will be no rain!" To say that to a king—and such a king! Imagine Ahab's furious reaction.

Narrate verses 2–7 as dramatically as possible. Describe his flight, imagine a hiding place in some caves perhaps and elicit from the children his feelings of fear, hunger, despair turning to joy and thankfulness when the ravens provide his food. And then the brook dried up. How would Elijah feel now?

2. Sometimes God lets us go through hard times. Elijah certainly did; he could no longer stay in his safe hiding place but had to travel north to a village called Zarephath on the Mediterranean shore, some distance north of Galilee. Here something happened which was to test Elijah's faith in God—and also that of a poor widow.

What are the children's reactions to tests? Do they like them? What do they prove? Elijah's test was a stiff one, one where he was asked if his faith (trust in God) was big enough to promise to another person what God had miraculously given to him at the Brook of Cherith in the previous verses, i.e. food when there was none around. Tell the story contained in verses 8–16. The prophet was triumphant. He even had faith to ask that the widow give him some food first! Explain that it was the custom for a man or a visitor to be fed first and Elijah was both! Was he showing that to his God this situation was nothing out of the ordinary?

This story lends itself to acting later so it will be helpful to emphasize emotions at varying stages of the story:

(a) Elijah's when he first said "Don't worry".
(b) The widow's when he said, "First make a loaf for me".
(c) Her son's when he saw his "last meal" going to the prophet.
(d) . . . when the food lasted on and on?

3. How do the pupils feel when they receive a long-awaited gift (calculator, bicycle?) and it is broken in the first few days? How would Mum or Dad feel if the new car were dented on its first day out?

How would the widow feel when her son, whose life had just been miraculously spared by God's provision of food, fell ill and died? It might be effective just to read verses 17–24. Just as Elijah had been tested after the miracle at Cherith, so the woman was being tested after her amazing experience with the flour and the oils. Have the children ever said, "Why?". Note that when the mother first cried out that question (verse 18), the prophet did not know the answer (verse 20). It was she herself who provided it in verse 24, "Now I know that you are a man of God and that the Lord really speaks through you!"

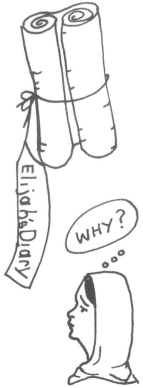

OPTIONAL ACTIVITIES

1. Have the children choose any episode and draw a picture with as much action or feeling as possible. Each could then hold it up and ask the question which must have been in the subject's mind, e.g. "Why did you let it happen, God?" Class discussion of answers.

2. Make a "Why and How" frieze with the above pictures, marking the questions boldly with felt tip pens. It is not necessary to discuss the

answers—at all costs, avoid glibness. It is enough for the children to know that there *was* an answer.

3. Have some pupils pair off to prepare (and later act out) an interview between their favourite television newscaster and Elijah. This could also be done for creative writing.
4. Groups may prepare and act out the whole dramatic story.
5. Older children may discuss more recent parallels of provision, e.g. Dr Barnardo, Tear Fund, Oxfam, etc.

Lesson 2   Elijah and the Prophets of Baal

1 Kings 18

AIM

To show that God expects his people to take a bold stand for right against wrong.
To show how God proved his power to many people through the faithfulness of one person.

INTRODUCTION

"Leave him alone! You know what he said he would do if he caught you!"
"Take my advice and stay where you are."
"Well, all I say is that I hope you come back in one piece. Rather you than me!"
Have the children even been given these warnings—or given them to anyone else? Discuss their experiences and suggestions and show that while sometimes it may be sound advice, at other times it may be wrong.

SUGGESTED PROCEDURE

God said to Elijah, "Go and present yourself to King Ahab . . . and I will send rain". I wonder how many friends said to the prophet, "Don't go!". Remind the children about the king's cruelty and evil practices.

43

This is surely one of the most dramatic stories in the whole Bible, one which will benefit from being presented as straight narrative. It is advisable to make sure of your facts from the whole chapter. Plan carefully, thinking out your additional details, included to heighten effect, and if possible practise beforehand.

Four sections become clear as we read.

1. The servant Obadiah's search for water, his fear on meeting Elijah, his description of Ahab's and Jezebel's activities and his eventual acquiescence. This is contained in verses 3–15. Make much of Elijah's promise in the last verse: "By the Lord Almighty whom I serve, I **promise** that I will present myself to the king that day".

   How important is it to keep a promise? Was it the same for Elijah?

2. Verses 16–29. "So there you are—the worst troublemaker in Israel!" So said Ahab to the prophet.

   "I'm not the troublemaker. *You* are!" So said Elijah to King AHAB! Have a few quick suggestions of the evil king's explosive reaction to that and then go on to describe the challenge to a contest (verses 19–24), whichever god sends fire is the real God! Verses 25–29 lend themselves to a humorous approach—make the most of it.

3. Elijah's part in the story is more serious (verses 30–40) with a slow, steady build-up towards the climax. Use the repetition ("Do it again. Do it once more.") to achieve this and when the fire falls have the children participate in the great "The Lord is God; the Lord alone is God!".

   Whether or not to include verse 40 depends on the level of understanding of the pupils. Some may easily see it to be the necessary eradication of an evil influence, but, without some previous knowledge of Old Testament principles, it is a difficult concept to grasp.

4. Verses 41–46 can be told briefly, yet even here there is a considerable feeling of tension as Elijah says **seven** times, "Go and look". **Six** times the servant returned with, "I didn't see anything". The culmination is in the last two verses when the wind begins to blow and the rain begins to fall. Describe Elijah's relief (he was after all very human) and convey to the class the humour of the closing pictures.

OPTIONAL ACTIVITIES

1. Ask some of the class to paint a large background frieze with very dry ground, a very blue sky and an altar. Have about two-thirds of the class paint "a frenzied figure" and build up the hysterical scene of Baal's followers pleading for fire. Each child may cut out and superimpose his own contribution. A small part at the end may be Elijah's altar leaping into flames.

Collage: bright bold colours with tissue paper : paint : mosaics : Stick on slithers of sandstone for altar stones : felt or plasticine for sacrifice : tissue flames.

2. Pupils may write out in large writing Elijah's words in verse 15 or verses 36 and 37. Ask them to cut these into jigsaw shapes and pass on to a neighbour to refit together.
3. Write Elijah's diary for that day.
4. Where did Elijah get the water for the trenches? Discuss. The present Mount Carmel is at Haifa on the Mediterranean Sea.

Lesson 3   Elijah, Fiery but Fearful

1 Kings 19:1–21; 2 Kings 2:1–18

AIM

To show that:
(a) even the strongest person has moments of weakness when he feels "down" or in despair.
(b) God understands these feelings and cares in a very practical way.

INTRODUCTION

It is well within the experience of the older child (though perhaps briefly) to "wish he were dead", or to be so afraid that he does not know what to do or where to turn for help. Discuss with the class any time when they have "wished they'd never been born". Be prepared for some frivolous answers but there will be serious ones too—at their own level of understanding or sensitivity. Not everyone will take part. In fact those with big problems may not but by our own comments and attitude we should have alerted the children to the fact that it is normal and not at all cowardly.

SUGGESTED PROCEDURE

Lead into the story of Elijah, who after the last two lessons will appear to be fearless and fiery.

(a) Elijah wants to die!

(b) Elijah finds a friend.

(c) Elijah disappears!

1. 1 Kings 19:1–18 "May I myself die if I haven't killed you by this time tomorrow!"—so speaks the wicked Jezebel and strikes fear into the brave prophet. He flees for his life. Tell the story dramatically; it starts slowly and quietly, moves on through the gentle encounter with the angel who gave such understanding and practical care, and gradually rises to a pitch with "the furious wind that split the hills and shattered the rocks". Much of the emphasis of the story will be lost if the narrator does not make varied use of voice and tone to portray changes of speed, mood and emotions. Sound effects on tape could be helpful here. After the climax of noise, the narrative subsides but intensifies in the quietness as the "soft whisper of God's voice" says, "Elijah, what are you doing here?" The prophet makes his complaint again and God encourages him to get up and get on with his work. (Note that he said this only after he had provided food and rest.) So instead of dying, he has to carry on the fight for good over evil (verses 15–19).

2. No longer does Elijah have to stand completely on his own. Talk briefly about "friends". Do the children like to have them? Do they need them? What do they do for us and vice versa? Do the advantages outweigh the occasional quarrels and hurts that arise?

   Apply some of this to the prophet's experience in verses 19–21 where Elisha is given to him. The Bible deals briefly with the incident but it is important nevertheless to bring the factual account into the context of real life.

3. 2 Kings 2:1–18. At this point, the emphasis shifts to Elisha. Try to do this in your own words, showing how God's call to service, and the power given to Elijah, was now transferred to his successor. It is not necessary to make this a lengthy description; the point will be driven home more dramatically by a straight brief narration followed by some spontaneous artwork.

OPTIONAL ACTIVITIES

1. Have art materials ready to do some work while in the mood of the story. Paint might be better than crayon or felt tips in that the result is more immediate.

- Circle from marg. top.
- Fill with polyfilla
- Scrape out (when dry) picture.
- paint.
- Stick on hanger on the back.

There is only one God and Jehovah is his name

Mt. CARMEL

2. Make a tape of sound effects incorporating the angel's voice, God's voice, the wind, the earthquake and the fire. (Use percussion instruments, crinkling paper, etc.) At a later date have the children retell the story making use of this.
3. Looking back over Elijah's life, ask the children to design a medal incorporating a motto and significant symbols.
4. Make use of this word square to review the story. Words are printed horizontally or vertically, moving up or down, to left or right. There are 35 words; for the teacher's benefit, these are:

1. Elijah	13. Obadiah	25. angel
2. Ahab	14. Carmel	26. earthquake
3. Jezebel	15. altar	27. wind
4. rain	16. Baal	28. Elisha
5. Cherith	17. prophet	29. oxen
6. ravens	18. knives	30. cloak
7. Zarephath	19. trench	31. courage
8. widow	20. promise	32. despair
9. son	21. fire	33. fearless
10. oil	22. cloud	34. bull
11. miracle	23. chariot	35. chariot
12. life	24. cave	(a second one)

X (except for one) does not count.
Simpler examples may be made for younger classes.

E	L	I	C	C	A	R	M	E	L	X	B	A	A	L
Z	O	J	A	L	L	I	A	L	T	P	F	E	A	R
A	I	A	V	E	E	F	X	X	A	R	S	S	E	L
R	L	H	E	G	R	A	I	N	R	O	B	A	H	A
E	X	X	A	N	E	A	R	C	E	M	X	R	X	X
P	H	A	T	H	X	X	T	H	S	I	X	A	X	P
W	S	O	N	B	O	E	H	E	R	I	X	V	E	R
I	X	X	X	U	B	K	Q	X	E	T	M	K	N	O
D	O	W	C	L	A	A	U	W	L	H	I	N	S	P
C	D	X	L	L	D	I	J	I	I	X	R	I	V	H
H	E	R	O	F	O	A	E	N	S	X	A	T	E	E
A	S	I	U	I	X	H	Z	D	H	A	C	R	S	T
R	P	A	D	R	E	X	E	B	E	L	L	E	X	X
I	X	H	C	E	N	C	L	O	A	K	E	N	C	H
O	T	A	R	I	O	T	C	O	U	R	A	G	E	X

NEHEMIAH

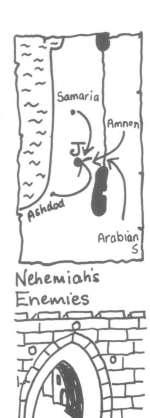

Nehemiah's
Enemies

HISTORICAL NOTE

Jerusalem is a very old city dating possibly from before 2000 B.C. It has for long held a special place in the hearts of the people of Israel. King David made it his capital and there the Temple was built. Throughout the centuries it was subject to attack. In 597 B.C. the armies of Nebuchadnezzar laid siege to the city and carried off its king to Babylon. In 586 B.C. the Temple was destroyed and the Jews taken captive to Babylon. Cyrus II of Persia took Babylon in 539 B.C. by which time the Persian Empire was at its height. It was his policy to allow subject peoples to follow their own religion and customs. So it came about that in 536 B.C. some Jews were allowed to return to Jerusalem to rebuild the city and Temple. Nehemiah was one such returned exile. Under his leadership the walls of Jerusalem were rebuilt.

The captivity marked the displeasure of God with his people for their sins. Many of the psalms express the people's longing to return to their own land.

The theme recurring throughout Nehemiah's memoirs is his dependence on God as shown by his frequent prayers. His consciousness of being constantly in God's company comes over very strongly.

JERUSALEM

Lesson 1   Setting the Scene

AIM

To show the important part played by Jerusalem in the life and aspirations of the Jews.

INTRODUCTION

In view of the importance of Jerusalem through the ages as well as its relevance to the story of Nehemiah it is worth while spending some considerable time on a study of the city. Have photographs and slides of present-day Jerusalem if possible but emphasize that the present city is physically different in many ways from the ancient city. Nevertheless there is much in the way of life that is similar—and there is a wall with its many gates, not the same wall and gates as Nehemiah's, it's true, but a photograph of one of the gates of the Jerusalem of today can bring to life the many references in the Bible to activities that took place at "the gate of the city". Using reference books children should find out what they can about its history.

SUGGESTED PROCEDURE

The main steps in the story are:

1. *Exile in Babylon*
   Tell briefly the story of the captivity as outlined in the Historical Note. Help the children to enter imaginatively into the feelings of the exiles.

What might they miss most in their new land? (What would the pupils miss most about their own town/country if they had to leave?) Psalm 137 gives poignant expression to their grief while Psalms 74, 79 and 80 are prayers for the nation's restoration.

A sketch-map showing Jerusalem, Babylon, the Persian Empire, Susa and the River Euphrates, would be useful.

2. *The Return*

Nehemiah 1; 2; 4; 6:15–19; 7; 12:27–43. The story can be told or read.

Questions to ask the children might be:

Chapter 1. In Nehemiah's prayer (verses 5–11).

(a) Why was it that the Jews were sent into exile? (verses 1–8).

(b) What promise had God given to them? (verse 9).

(c) What special request did Nehemiah make?

Chapter 2

(d) How did God answer his prayer in Nehemiah 1:11?

(e) Look at verse 4. What might his prayer have been? (It must have been very short—"Lord, give me the right words", "Lord, help me".)

(f) What were the names of his two enemies?

(g) Why was Nehemiah so confident that he could rebuild the walls?

OPTIONAL ACTIVITIES

Each child could do a large silhouette-style picture of the midnight inspection. The background paper could be dark blue. They could cut out a building from black paper and stick it on. Nehemiah on his donkey and his friends should be cut out of black paper of a different texture or dark grey paper could be used. Overlap as appropriate.

Lesson 2   Into Action

Nehemiah 4 and 6

AIM

To tell about the rebuilding of the city wall.

SUGGESTED PROCEDURE

1. From Chapter 3 it can be seen that the project was carried forward in a very methodical and workmanlike way. However there was opposition in the form of:
   (a) ridicule (4:2–3);
   (b) a plot to attack Jerusalem and create confusion (4:7);
   (c) an attempt to lure Nehemiah away from Jerusalem (6:2);
   (d) an unsealed letter (and who could resist a peep inside) spreading false rumours (6:6);
   (e) an attempt to ruin his reputation (6:13).
2. Have the children note Nehemiah's response to each attack:
   (a) He prayed and kept on working (4:4);
   (b) He prayed and kept men on guard (4:9, 16);
   (c) "I am doing important work and can't go down there" (6:3);
   (d) He prayed, "But now, God, make me strong!" and he went on working (6:9);
   (e) He prayed and went on working (6:14).
3. *Dedication of the Wall* (7:1–3; 12:27–43)
   After 52 days the task was completed. Describe the procession—two groups marching in opposite directions on top of the wall and meeting in the temple area. The sound of music and rejoicing could be heard far and wide.
   Nehemiah's combination of work and prayer led to a successful and happy restoration.

OPTIONAL ACTIVITIES

1. Discussion: Children find ridicule difficult to bear. Can the children remember times when they were subjected to it or subjected others to it? How do they react to it? Any ideas for helping others cope with it? Stress how wrong and cheap it is to ridicule others.
2. Describe the strategy Nehemiah adopted (Chapter 6) for warding off an attack while at the same time getting on with the work.
3. Drama: Chapters 4 and 6 lend themselves to drama.
4. Music and movement: Make up music (using what percussion instruments you have and adapting everyday objects) for the procession and then work out a movement routine to express the joy and thanksgiving of the occasion.
5. Read: Psalms 87, 122, 125 and 126 which are relevant to this period in Israel's history.

ESTHER

Esther 1–10

AIM

To show how God can interweave the circumstances of an individual with those of a complete nation to effect his own plans (although God's name is not mentioned in the story!).

To tell the children a fast-flowing enjoyable Bible story, both tragic and humorous.

INTRODUCTION

For an understanding of this book it is necessary first to sketch in some historical background.

Many years before, the Jews had been captured by the Babylonians and although some time previous to the happenings of this story many thousands had been allowed home, a large number would clearly have remained where they had settled. It was now the Persian Empire with King Xerxes (5th century B.C.) at the height of his power. He ruled over "one hundred and twenty-seven provinces all the way from India to Sudan" (Esther 1:1).

The tale of Esther, the Jewess, relates how God thwarted a plan to massacre her entire nation. It is the background to the festival of "Purim" (the lots cast to determine the day to be set for the mass murder). The festival is still celebrated—see Optional Activities.

The chief characters are:

Xerxes, the Persian king with his many palaces, wives and great wealth.
Mordecai, a Jew but a high official at the Persian Court in Susa.
Esther, his cousin whose Jewish name was Hadassah.
Haman, the king's chief minister and the villain of the story.

This narrative in a modern translation lends itself to reading aloud, but it is advisable to do this only in part. It is necessary for the teacher to be familiar with the following details which (although presented here as one unit) may easily be serialized. Incorporate as much of the colourful detail as possible.

SUGGESTED PROCEDURE

1. Esther 1. King Xerxes gives a long-lasting banquet and a huge display of his extreme wealth. Queen Vashti refuses to leave her own feast in the women's quarters to "be shown off" to her husband and his drunken friends. The queen is banished and a proclamation to this effect is sent throughout all the provinces with their different languages and forms of writing—a mammoth task in itself!

2. Esther 2:1–18. Girls are brought in from all over the provinces for a year's special beauty treatment before entering the king's presence. At this point introduce Mordecai who had adopted Hadassah (Esther) and now put her forward for the contest. Esther is chosen to be queen in place of Vashti and a holiday is proclaimed throughout the empire! It is kept secret that she is Jewish and related to Mordecai.

3. Esther 2:19–23. Mordecai uncovers a plot to kill the king and thus saves his life.

4. Esther 3. Introduce Haman whose power quickly "goes to his head". Relate dramatically his fury at Mordecai for refusing to bow down to him and describe his plans to kill every Jew in the Persian Empire (verse 6).

   He casts lots (purim) to set the day for the massacre. The king receives a distorted story about "the insubordination of a certain race" and gives his official stamp to the already-prepared proclamation. Once again, runners have to run far and wide!

5. Esther 4:1–17; 5:1–4. Mordecai hears of the plan and pleads with his cousin to help. She finally agrees to go unasked into the king's presence, thereby risking her life, but she does it for the sake of her people. All the Jews meanwhile fast and pray.

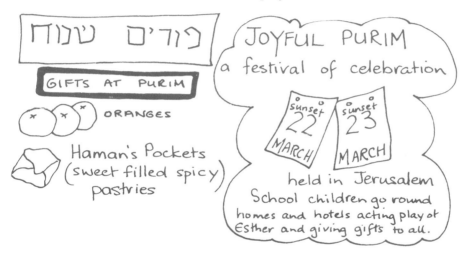

Xerxes accepts Esther and offers her the proverbial "half of his kingdom" . . . but she asks merely that he and Haman will come to a special banquet.

6. Esther 5:5–14. Haman has a good time and is especially delighted to be invited to come back again the next night to yet another party. On the way home his enjoyment is marred by rage at being ignored by Mordecai. His wife and friends suggest a twenty-two metres high gallows for his enemy. This plan set underway, he goes to bed happy.

7. Esther 6. To while away a sleepless night, the king has the palace records read to him and thus hears about Mordecai's act of loyalty in saving his life; he consults Haman for advice about "how to treat someone very special with the greatest honour possible". The prime minister, thinking the king is referring to him, suggests what he himself would most like (verses 7–9). Haman's misery is acute at having to follow through his own suggestions—for Mordecai!

8. Esther 7. During the second banquet Esther reveals the plot to destroy her people and the king leaves the room in a fury that any traitor, particularly Haman, should do such a thing. Haman "throws himself on Esther's couch to plead for mercy" (verse 8) and is discovered there by the king. He is hanged on his own gallows.

9. Esther 8 to 10. This section may be omitted or passed over quickly. Haman's property is given to Esther who confesses that Mordecai is her cousin. He is welcomed to court and given power.

   The queen pleads for the Jews and yet another proclamation is sent to the provinces. This one cancels the previous one and allows the Jews to defend themselves when necessary. There is great rejoicing (Esther 8:15–17).

   The Jews' enemies are destroyed and the festival of Purim is established.

OPTIONAL ACTIVITIES

1. Find a map of the Persian Empire and trace some of its vastness. Find out a little about it and make drawings of their beautiful mosaics, their dark red, black painted pottery depicting simple birds and animals, their gold drinking cups with animals moulded at the base.

2. Have a discussion on the character traits displayed by the chief characters (courage, treachery, selfishness, greed, etc.) and encourage application to the children's own experience.

3. Tell the children that the Feast of Purim is still celebrated today by the Jewish community. It is a happy celebration in spring where the story is read aloud in the synagogue and the people shout, shake rattles and ring bells whenever Haman's name is mentioned! The children can retell the story in this way.

   There is also an opportunity here to play Israeli music. Records are easily available and music from "Fiddler on the Roof" may be used.

4. Use the story to foster a sensitive approach to minority groups. Speak about the Jews, scattered throughout the world yet retaining their own distinct, national identity, religion and traditions. Mention some of their persecutions and discuss these thoughtfully. The children could identify with Anne Frank for example.

5. Divide the class into groups and the story into sections. Give each group time to prepare one section and act it out. The story lends itself to drama.

6. Make a large book (zig-zag or ring-backed) telling the story in picture and prose (or poetry?).

7. Esther was very brave. Find other such courageous women and discover something about their lives.

ESTHER has cooked all the King's favourite dishes, Kasha, potato and liver-filled Knishes. Kreplach and kugels just fit for a king—These are a few of his favourite things! ♪ ♫ ♪ ♪ ♫
CHICKEN soup eaten with kneydlach or noodles, stuffed cabbage, stuffed peppers, stuffed fruit-filled strudels, Fricasses made from the best chicken wings — All of his majesty's favourite things! ♫ ♪ ♪
THEY are all eating, they are drinking —only ESTHER's sad. The King asks her why, she reveals Haman's plot —Now poor Haman feels so bad! ♪ ♫ ♪ ♪
SONG FOR PURIM to tune Favourite Things/Sound of Music

THE BOOK OF PSALMS

BACKGROUND NOTE

The Book of Psalms forms part of the writings of the Hebrew Scriptures. They are often called "the Psalms of David", partly because David was a skilled player on the lyre and known as "the sweet psalmist of Israel", partly because he was regarded by the Jews as the real founder of the Temple where these sacred songs were collected and sung. It is true also that David's name stands at the head of a good many of them, though that does not necessarily mean that he was the author.

The collection of one hundred and fifty psalms in our Bible is divided into five books, each group closing with a doxology. The groups are: 1–41; 42–72; 73–89; 90–106; 107–150. Probably this division was to conform to the Pentateuch or five books of the Law, but it was nothing to do with the date of the psalms or with particular themes. The longest psalm (119) is in the form of an acrostic in which each section of eight verses begins with a letter of the Hebrew alphabet. Every verse has a reference to the "law" or a synonym such as "testimony".

The Psalms were composed over a long period of time, covering most of the triumphs and disasters of Hebrew history. They take many forms and have different purposes in the circle of the year's worship in the Temple at Jerusalem. Here are some of them:

1. Psalms to be chanted on public and national occasions (e.g. 2, 18, 20, 132).
2. Psalms to be sung by the Temple choirs (e.g. 47, 93, 96–99).
3. Psalms for pilgrims to the holy city (e.g. 84).
4. Psalms to accompany animal sacrifice in the sanctuary (e.g. 113–118).
5. Songs of seed-time and harvest (e.g. 67).

6. Psalms for other days of festival (e.g. 120–134).

7. Psalms which are prayers for private devotion (e.g. 4, 16, 23, 30).

We have little information about the form of Temple worship so long ago, except that annual festivals were held there and the daily sacrifice of animals with appropriate prayer and praise, so it is not always possible to decide what each psalm was originally used for, or to which group it should belong.

Great is the Lord and greatly to be praised.... Ps 145

AIM

To familiarize the pupils with some of the content of the Book of Psalms, many of them written by King David.

INTRODUCTION

Refer to hymns and psalms that are sung in church or school and discuss why they are part of our worship.

SUGGESTED PROCEDURE

1. From the information contained in the Background Note summarize the main points.
2. From the examples given (1–7) select one or two psalms to read out and relate them to the theme suggested. Choose unfamiliar ones as well as a familiar one like "The Lord is my shepherd" (Psalm 23).
3. Relate some of the psalms to hymns which have been more recently written for occasions like Christmas, Easter and Harvest.

OPTIONAL ACTIVITIES

1. Sing or read some of the well-known psalms to show how beautiful the language is.
2. Select a verse from a psalm and illustrate it.

The sun comes out in the morning like a happy bridegroom

God made a home for the sun

like an athlete eager to run a race

it starts at one end of the sky and goes across to the other

Psalm 19 v 4a

3. Play a recording of psalms sung or narrated (e.g. David Kossoff or Laurence Olivier).
4. Play a recording of psalms sung in Hebrew. Discuss the place of psalms in Jewish worship today and perhaps visit a synagogue.

THE BOOK OF PROVERBS

BACKGROUND NOTE

The Book of Proverbs is a collection of wise sayings, forming, with Job and Ecclesiastes, the Wisdom Literature of Hebrew Scriptures. These maxims are mainly concerned with the moral education of the young, whose training has always been an important part of Jewish life.

The book was probably made up after the Exile from a number of earlier sources. Solomon was famous for his wise sayings, so the whole work is named after him. But it would be impossible to pin down proverbial sayings to one time or one man, and though some may come from Solomon, others can be traced to an Egyptian source.

AIM

To introduce the Book of Proverbs and relate some of them to present-day proverbs.

INTRODUCTION

Quote some well-known modern proverbs and discuss both their origin and meaning.

SUGGESTED PROCEDURE

1. From the notes above summarize the background to the Book of Proverbs in the Bible.
2. Select a few proverbs and discuss what they might mean, e.g.
   (a) 3:5–6
   (b) 11:17
   (c) 15:1
   (d) 17:22
   (e) 20:4
   (f) 30:24–28
   There are many more!
3. Compare and contrast the Book of Proverbs with some modern proverbs.
4. A lot of proverbs speak about wisdom. Discuss the subtle difference between knowledge and wisdom. How can we be wise in what we do? Reference might be made to the "wise and foolish" parables of Jesus.
5. Many proverbs look at the world of nature. What can we learn by looking at the world around us?

OPTIONAL ACTIVITIES

1. Children could write out or display a proverb from the Bible and write a modern equivalent. Make use of the humorous illustrations in the *Good News Bible*.
2. With illustrations from nature write out related proverbs and display alongside.
3. Read the story or make a play based on one or two of the proverbs.

THREE FRIENDS OF DANIEL

Daniel 3

AIM

To tell about God's protection of three men who were faithful to their beliefs.

INTRODUCTION

Most children will be aware of the story of Daniel in the Lion's Den. This story is about three of Daniel's friends in Babylon. The incident happened before his experience in the den.

SUGGESTED PROCEDURE

Vividly retell the story. Here are some of the main points.

1. Recall that the Jews were in exile in Babylon, a country with a strange language and a different religion. Despite this, some of the Jews had adapted to life there, without compromising their faith, and were well thought of by some of the leaders of the country. Daniel was greatly respected by King Nebuchadnezzar (Daniel 2:48–9) and was put into a position of authority. At Daniel's request, three young men, Shadrach, Meshach and Abednego, were also appointed to work with him.
2. Explain about the huge golden image of the king which was set up in Babylon and the decree which went out through the land that everyone should bow down and worship it whenever the sound of particular music was heard. The penalty for disobedience, which implied disrespect for the king, was death by fire.
3. Explain why Daniel's friends could not obey this decree as it directly challenged one of the Commandments of the Jewish people, that they should "not bow down to any idol".
4. Recount how they were seen to walk past the statue by some of their enemies who reported the matter to Nebuchadnezzar. Brought before the king, they still refused to obey and explained why. Threatened with death in the furnace, they told the king that they would be faithful to God to whom they would pray for deliverance.

Map of Middle East golden statue from Mod-Roc-sprayed with gold paint pipe cleaner people.

paper mâché utensils
fruit and food for banquet.

MEDIA

Babylon

PERSIA

Jerusalem

Daniel exiled in the court of Babylon

5. Tell of the king's anger and his command to heat the furnace seven times greater than normal. It was so hot that even the men who threw them into the fire died in the process. Try to capture the drama of the scene as the king and the others around him looked in amazement as the victims were seen to be walking around inside the furnace. Indeed, there seemed to be a fourth person with them!

6. The king shouted out and told them to come out of the fire and they emerged unscathed. Confused, but full of respect for Shadrach, Meshach and Abednego, he then made a new decree to the effect that the young men were to be promoted and their God was to be honoured.

7. Discuss the men's faithfulness to God and to their beliefs and willingness to take a stand in the face of opposition, even if they faced death. They did not know that they would be saved, and there are many occasions when people in the Bible have suffered hardship and death for their faith. You may wish to refer at this point to people in history who have suffered and died for their beliefs. God calls on many people to suffer and face persecution and only a few of them may be delivered, if at all.

OPTIONAL ACTIVITIES

1. Dramatize the story. Suitable scenery might be a polystyrene model of the golden image, fluorescent or crepe paper for fire, etc.

2. Set up and record an imaginary interview with the three men after their ordeal; or let the children write an eye-witness account of the climax of the story.

3. Prayer: "Lord, help us to stand up for what we believe is good and right even in the face of danger. Be with all those who today throughout the world are faced with difficult choices as they serve you".

THE STORY OF JONAH

GENERAL AIM

To help the children to understand that God loves all people equally.

Lesson 1   The Man Who Ran Away from God

AIM

To introduce the story of Jonah—a man who *tried* to run away from God.

INTRODUCTION

Ask the class to give examples of ways in which children react when asked by parents to do something they do not wish to do, e.g. pretend not to hear; become very busy with other things; go out of earshot.

SUGGESTED PROCEDURE

1. Introduce Jonah as a prophet—a man who had promised to tell other people about God and give them his message.
2. Fill in the background briefly. He lived long before Jesus but in the same land of Israel. The people there believed in God and thought he loved them exclusively. Nineveh was the capital city of Assyria, a very large nation who did not believe in the God of Israel. They were the enemies of Israel.

3. Talk about God's command to Jonah. He had to go and tell the people of Nineveh that if they weren't sorry for all the wrong things they had done and didn't stop doing them, God would punish them. Jonah did not want to go! Ask the children to suggest the reasons for his reluctance, e.g. "He was afraid"; "Nineveh was a long way from home."; "They would not listen to him", etc. Raise the possibility that the real reason was that he wanted them to be punished! This will become apparent as the story develops.

4. The situation is too much for Jonah and he runs away. Ask the children how they imagine God might feel at this point. Sad? Angry? Disappointed?

5. Jonah boards a ship at Joppa and goes below to hide. If you have a map of this area show the relative positions of Joppa, Tarshish (probably Spain) and Nineveh. Point out that Nineveh was in the opposite direction from Tarshish.

6. We are told that God sent a storm at sea to make Jonah return and go to Nineveh. Retell this story dramatically or, with older children read straight from a modern translation. The main points are:
Severity of storm; fear of sailors who throw cargo overboard to lighten the ship; they pray to the gods they believe in—all to no avail. The sailors are angry to find Jonah asleep! They tell him to pray to his god that the ship should be saved. (Would Jonah want to pray?) When they question this stranger they find out who he is and what he was trying to do. Emphasize the reaction and fear of these superstitious seamen when he tells them he has broken a promise to his god—"The God of Heaven who made land and *sea*", Jonah tells them.

7. Reluctantly the sailors throw Jonah overboard to the mercy of the waves. Compare the sailors' attitude to that of Jonah towards the people of Nineveh.
There is immediate calm, much to the sailors' surprise.

8. Try to capture the fear of Jonah as he struggles in the water watching the ship disappear out of sight and the terror when he is swallowed whole by a huge fish, which the story tells us was provided by God.

9. Still alive inside the fish he realizes how foolish he has been and wishes that his life would not end in this way. He couldn't live long surely in this dark, horrible place. If only he could have a second chance, he would go to Nineveh! Dramatically describe the surprise when the fish ejects him and he is cast up on to a deserted beach, bruised, sore and burned by the acids in the fish's stomach . . . but glad to be alive!

Jonah's Prayer

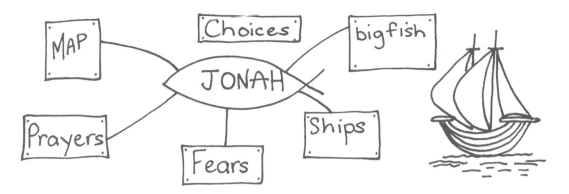

OPTIONAL ACTIVITIES

1. Art: Storm at sea; frieze of sea creatures; humorous drawing of Jonah inside the fish.
2. Dramatize the conversation between Jonah and the sailors.
3. Research into types of ships and cargoes in these days perhaps related to maps of the Eastern Mediterranean area then and now.
4. Reading of Jonah's prayer (Jonah 2).
5. Make up a prayer giving thanks for God's goodness, forgiveness and protection.
6. Hymns: "When I needed a neighbour were you there" (*Someone's Singing, Lord*); "O Jesus I have promised"; "Saviour teach me day by day."
7. Talk about the meaning of the common expression "He is a proper Jonah" in relation to the story so far.

Lesson 2   The Man Who Disagreed with God

AIM

To continue the story of Jonah and to encourage children to care when others are in trouble through wrong-doing.

INTRODUCTION

Recap main points of Lesson 1.

SUGGESTED PROCEDURE

1. Tell how Jonah eventually decides to keep his promise and goes to Nineveh to warn the people there that they will be punished if they do not change their ways. Picture him entering the city, looking perhaps for the centre or market place where the people are likely to be.
2. Describe the crowds gathering round this strange foreigner with an even stranger message. Think of Jonah's surprise when they heed his warnings and decide to fast and pray to his God for forgiveness and to change their ways.
3. Elicit from the children how they think God might feel about this. Discuss briefly how we might feel when people change their behaviour for the better. Do we encourage them or do we doubt their sincerity?

Jonah runs away....

Jonah prays

Jonah gets 2nd chance !!

Jonah learns a hard lesson

61

4. Describe Jonah's reaction. He is unhappy and angry for he really wanted God to destroy his enemy. This is their God, surely he had no right to love and forgive the enemies of Israel. What about all they had done? One can forgive, but can one forget?

5. Talk about Jonah's departure from the city still thinking that God will punish the people of Nineveh and not really believing that they meant what they said. Deep down he is angry with God.

6. Go on to tell the strange story about the large plant where Jonah sought shelter from the burning sun (remember he was still suffering from sores after his ordeal at sea and inside the fish). To his surprise the plant, the only place of shade around, withers and dies. Ask the children how he might feel at this point. The Bible says he was angry with the plant! Go on to tell how God points out to him (Jonah 4:10–11 may be read out) that the plant was not grown by Jonah, nor did he care for it yet he is sorry and angry! How much more should he pity Ninevah where there are living people who need compassion.

7. The narrative ends there but children may wish to imagine how Jonah felt after hearing these final words and what action he may have taken.

OPTIONAL ACTIVITIES

1. Make a class concertina book illustrating the main points of the story.
2. Plants of the desert could be illustrated and discussed.
3. The discussion on attitudes to other people, selfishness, etc. could be developed.
4. Songs: "Far Round the World" *(The Church Hymnary)*; "Cross over the Road" *(BBC)*; "Can you Count the Stars? *(Someone's Singing, Lord)*; "Remember all the People." *(Sing to God)*.
5. Make up a prayer about caring for others.
6. If started in the previous lesson, extend the drama of the story.

NEW TESTAMENT

THE CHRISTMAS STORY

Luke 2:1–20; Matthew 1:18–25; 2:1–23

INTRODUCTORY NOTE

It is always difficult to consider a different approach to these familiar events. However, we suggest that you look at these happenings as they affected the main characters in the story. The angels brought the message, "Peace". What did "peace" mean to each of these people and what effect did the birth of Jesus have on their lives?

Lesson 1   The Shepherds

AIM

To tell the main events of the Christmas story as viewed by the shepherds.

INTRODUCTION

Refer to "peace talks" that go on in the world, perhaps looking at articles or headlines from newspapers. Then read out the verse from the story— ". . . and on earth peace and goodwill . . .". Discuss briefly what the children think "peace" is. Quietness? The countryside? No wars? etc. Explain that we are going to consider what peace may have meant to the main characters in the Christmas story, looking first at the shepherds.

SUGGESTED PROCEDURE

1. Discuss what peace might have meant to the shepherds. The Israelites were originally a nation of shepherds, basically a peace-loving people. In history, from the events of the Exodus onwards, they had to be trained to fight against their enemies. Many times in their past they had been put under the authority of invading powers; now at this time in history they were under the heel of the Roman Empire. Bands of resistance fighters, called zealots, had grouped to annoy the Roman army. However, for the shepherds, this was not the path to peace; peace was getting on with their job without interruption; or again, getting a good price for the wool at the market.

2. Briefly go over the familiar events of this interruption to their peaceful shepherding on the hills; the bright light, the voices and singing of the angels. Discuss what their reaction might be to this disturbance. They would surely want to see this child who would bring a new kind of peace to the earth!

3. Consider the preparations they might make before they made their way to Bethlehem; ensuring the sheep were cared for; preparing food, etc. What would they talk about on their way to the stable? Perhaps the change that this child's life would have on Israel and more importantly on their lives.

4. Go on to describe their arrival at the stable, meeting Mary, Joseph and Jesus, telling them about the angels. What else might they have talked about?

5. Consider what they would discuss on the way back to their flock. Would they forget these events easily? Did they perhaps experience a new kind of peace after meeting Jesus?

OPTIONAL ACTIVITIES

1. Display the verse, "Peace on earth . . ." and below it put a newspaper cutting about peace talks.
2. Give children a number of short extracts to read out about war and trouble, followed by extracts describing peaceful events in the world today. Between each extract read out the verse from the Bible spoken to the shepherds.
3. Dramatize the scene in the fields, stressing the theme of peace.
4. Find pictures or illustrations showing tranquillity in the midst of turmoil, e.g. a flower in a busy town, a sleeping child in a noisy street.

5. As well as the familiar carols choose other songs on the theme of peace.
6. Ask children to write out what peace means to them and what changes they would like to see in the world today.

Lesson 2   The Wise Men

AIM

To explore the effect of Jesus' birth on the "Wise Men".

INTRODUCTION

Recall previous discussion on the theme of "Peace".

SUGGESTED PROCEDURE

1. Discuss briefly who the people described as the Wise Men may have been—astrologers, kings or leaders? Certainly rich, if the gifts are indications of wealth.
2. What might peace have meant to them in their positions of authority and wisdom? It may have meant prosperity and wealth enough to enjoy themselves, or perhaps peaceful government to allow them to handle trade and make money to use in the pursuit of peace. As leaders, peace would be linked to their control over others, commanding respect or at least submissiveness. As stargazers, peace might mean being assured that knowledge and guidance may be sought in the vastness of the heavens.

3. Discuss their curiosity and their quest for the king whose star they had seen in the sky, their long journey and their desire for information. Speculate on their thoughts as they travelled. Were they looking for someone who would bring peace to their world? Or were they considering fame or financial gain?
4. Recall:
   (a) their visit to Herod's palace (surely the place where one would normally find a king!);
   (b) their discussions with Herod (but not Herod's reactions at this point);
   (c) their eventual discovery of the child Jesus (not perhaps in the stable, as it is believed he may have been older by this time);
   (d) the warning that they were not to return to Herod.
5. Consider what effect these events may have had on their lives. Would they be surprised to find this important person in humble surroundings? What might they talk about to Mary and Joseph? On their way home what would they discuss? No doubt they too may have experienced a new understanding of peace. How would their lives be changed?

OPTIONAL ACTIVITIES

1. In addition to well-known Christmas songs explore the theme of peace in hymns, songs and poetry.
2. Dramatize the events as they affected the wise men, again stressing the theme of peace.
3. Write a story or report or tape a personal view of the events as told by one of the visitors, from the sighting of the star to the meeting with Jesus, describing his feelings and the change the event had on life.
4. Under the heading "Peace on earth . . ." build up a frieze illustrating the development of their search and discovery.

Lesson 3   Herod

AIM

To explore the events of Jesus' birth as they affected Herod.

INTRODUCTION

Fill in the background to the political situation in Herod's day. Tell about the Roman occupation of Palestine, the resistance, active and passive, of the inhabitants and the appointment of the ruthless Herod as a puppet king.

SUGGESTED PROCEDURE

1. Discuss what peace might mean to a man like Herod. Peace with the Romans meant doing what he was told, subduing the Jews and ensuring that no other leader took his place. Speak about the rising tide of public opinion against him, particularly worrying as he was well aware that he had no real right to the throne by appointment or heritage as far as the Jews were concerned.

2. Consider Herod's surprise and worry when the wise men visit him. What thoughts might he have had as he talked to them? He consulted his own sages and searched his records for the information he found in Micah 5:2. He asked the men to tell him when they found this special person so that he too could worship him.

3. Talk about the lack of peace that Herod would now have as he waited for the men to return and lead on to his devastating decision to kill all the young boys in the area to ensure the death of Jesus. Speak about God's protection of Jesus and his family.

4. How would Herod now feel? Contrast his experience with what it might have been if, like the shepherds and the wise men, he had looked for Jesus to worship him. Instead of peace he found trouble, fear and bewilderment. History records his ultimate downfall.

OPTIONAL ACTIVITIES

1. Dramatize the events, e.g. a peaceful village scene interrupted by the sudden arrival of Herod's soldiers.

2. Make a tape recording, radio documentary or a newspaper account of the meeting with the wise men and the dreadful event that followed.

3. Write Herod's diary of the events over these days, trying to capture his feelings and lack of peace.

Lesson 4   Mary and Joseph

AIM

To consider what the events surrounding the birth of Jesus might have meant to Mary and Joseph.

INTRODUCTION

Talk about what life was like for Mary and Joseph before these events took place: Mary, a young woman living at home, perhaps with her parents, and Joseph, a carpenter trying to a make a living in difficult times in Palestine.

SUGGESTED PROCEDURE

1. Discuss what peace would mean to the young couple, looking forward to their marriage and employment to support them. Peace also in the community in troubled times.

2. Describe, with reference to the Bible account, how they soon discovered that their lives were to be changed by the birth of Jesus.

3. What would their thoughts be:
   (a) as they journeyed to Bethlehem?
   (b) as they tried inn after inn?
   (c) when the different visitors came?
   (d) on being warned of Herod's evil plan?

   What kind of peace would they have to experience now? From then on their child would be the centre of discussion in the land; they had a great responsibility but with God's help and comforting words they experienced peace through it all.

4. Recalling the main topic of peace as portrayed in the preceding lessons, compare and contrast the outlook of each of the characters before and after they encountered Jesus. Did peace come to Palestine? History would say no, so had the angels message been false? Jesus was to bring inner peace to those who followed him.

5. Refer now to other people in the Bible whose lives were changed when they met Jesus: the disciples, Mary Magdalene, Zacchaeus, etc.

OPTIONAL ACTIVITIES

1. Make up a prayer about peace in our time; peace in the world and inner peace despite trouble in the world, found through the central person in the Christmas story.

2. Under the heading of the message given by the angels, add contrasting words of trouble and peace as they relate to the individuals, e.g. worry—calm; fear—joy; hatred—love.

3. Read about people in history who brought peace in troubled times through their faith and trust in God: David Livingstone, Mary Slessor, Florence Nightingale, Martin Luther King, William Wilberforce, Mother Teresa, etc.

JESUS GOES TO THE TEMPLE

Luke 2:41–52

AIM

To teach the story of Jesus being lost in the temple and to show that, as he was growing into manhood, he was beginning to realize who he was and what lay ahead of him.

INTRODUCTION

Nazareth was a busy little town lying south-west of the Sea of Galilee. There were many such places scattered around this Galilean province, populated by independent peoples (not all Jews) who often rebelled against their cruel masters, the Romans.

Imagine some villagers, just a few years before this story took place, curiously watching a small family coming very slowly up the steep road to their town. Why—it was Joseph, that fine young carpenter, with Mary, his young wife! And that lively youngster rushing ahead must be their first child!

Mary and Joseph had come back from Egypt to set up home in Nazareth (see Matthew 2:19–23).

SUGGESTED PROCEDURE

1. *Childhood*

    We know little of the actual boyhood of Jesus but we can guess a good deal from what he said and from stories that he told later on as he was "going about his Father's business". (Luke 2:49, Authorized Version.) It would be worthwhile at this point to spend a little time describing how Jesus:

    watched his mother fetching water, grinding corn and baking bread;

    studied his father's methods of making ploughs and furniture, etc.;

    played with other children, some of whom were happy and some of whom sulked! (Matthew 11:16–17);

    went to synagogue school and sat on the floor learning long scriptures by heart;

    watched the farmers at work and saw the birds swooping down. (Matthew 13:1–9);

    learned to recognize the signs of good and bad weather. (Matthew 16:2–3);

    helped shepherds to look for lost sheep (Luke 15:1–7) and knew about wolves (Matthew 10:16), foxes (Matthew 8:20) and birds (Matthew 10:29–30);

    climbed hills and looked beyond the traders passing along the road to the sparkling sea beyond;

    watched wedding and funeral processions (Matthew 11:17);

    saw folk bargaining in the market and discovered the awful differences between the rich and the miserably poor.

    Try to build up a lively, graphic picture of Jesus' childhood, a peaceful setting in the midst of surrounding violence—because he would also see his fellow Galileans flogged or sometimes even crucified by the Romans. Even as Jesus was growing up, his mind must have burned with questions reaching out to people and loving them as he did but hating the injustice and the wrong. Was he beginning to see that he was to love the world as his heavenly father did?

2. *Manhood at last!*

    Meanwhile Jesus had his twelfth birthday and was therefore considered almost grown up and fit to take his place amongst crowds from all parts of the land who would gather at Jerusalem for the Feast of the Passover. He must have been so pleased when his turn came to join the "Galilean caravan". (Explain this!)

    The journey would take a few days and excitement must have built high as they came closer to the City of David (Jesus knew his Jewish history very well). Perhaps he asked his parents endless questions as they journeyed on. The last 27 km climbed steeply up from Jericho and that part of the trail was usually enlivened by music with drums and cymbals as well as singing. The Mount of Olives would hide the great city from view but as they reached its summit the white marble buildings and golden-roofed temple would burst into sight. It has been called "The City of Gold and Snow". Picture Jesus, his hand holding the reins of his mother's donkey, still and gazing at the scene which had so

Collage of TEMPLE: use gold silver sweet paper + stone coloured sugar paper.

Altar of Sacrifice

TEMPLE

golden table with showbread

7 branched candlestick

Court of Priests

Court of Women

Beautiful Gate

Court of Gentiles

Merchant Money Changers

Teacher of Law

Priest

often been described to him. But they couldn't stay there all night. It was to be an early start the next day and the boy would have to help to build the booth of wicker or branches (home for a week), lay out the mats and light a fire. Friends and relations laughed and called out to each other as they recognized familiar faces. (Did any of the men talk worriedly about the political state of the land?) And then, in the open, Jesus might watch the setting sun flame over the golden city before he fell asleep.

3. *The Temple*

Not Solomon's one nor the later Jewish one but a magnificent edifice built by Herod the Great on the site of the others. Josephus, the historian, tells how the top of the hill was not big enough for his plans and he had to build mounds and fill in gullies to extend the area for his dream building. There were wonderful porticoes supported by pillars of immense, white, marble blocks and the roofs were adorned with cedar wood, fretwork and carvings. In the centre was the temple itself.

Describe the porch, the pillars past which no foreigner (gentile) could go. Did Jesus wonder why? Through a gold and silver gate he saw the temple itself—but he stayed under the cloisters because here he found the learned Rabbis who questioned and taught all those who gathered to listen. (Pictures of the temple are quite easily accessible for any teacher who wants to show a plan of the building.)

During these days, Jesus must have been the most attentive pupil. The Bible does not explain more about this but, with the children, imagine some of the questions racing around Jesus' mind—and the love, knowledge and fear of the future which may have exploded into dreadful realization at that time—because now Jesus may have been recognizing something of what he was going to do in later life.

4. *Going home*

The time came for the Jews to break up their booths and go back home with camels and asses heavily laden. Describe how Mary and Joseph would go, chatting and happy, and not at all worried that Jesus was not with them. But when night-time came, it was a different story. Build up a picture of the search, the panic and the return journey—it was not until the third day that they found him in the temple among the Rabbis, speaking as well as listening. Dramatize in your telling, the conversation of verses 48–50 and conjure up something of the feeling of mystery that must have been in his parents' mind. "Did you not know that I had to be in my father's house?"

And so they returned to Nazareth and for eighteen years we hear nothing except that Jesus "grew both in body and in wisdom, gaining favour with God and men". He lived an ordinary life in a carpenter's shop—but there was a secret and mysterious part too, which we shall only understand later on.

OPTIONAL ACTIVITIES

1. Have the children draw a cartoon strip telling the story. This can be done individually or built up as a class effort.
2. The story lends itself to dramatization in three parts:
   (a) the journey to Jerusalem;
   (b) the temple;
   (c) the search and discovery.
3. Set a painting competition. A caption could be written below. The camp site, the view of an eastern city and the temple scenes appeal to the children's imagination.
4. Find out something about the Jewish Bar Mitzvah ceremony of today for boys of thirteen.

JOHN THE BAPTIST

Don't beafraid Zecharian

Book of an UNUSUAL MAN

BIRTH
MAN
MESSAGE

INTRODUCTORY NOTE

John the Baptist is depicted as the immediate forerunner of Jesus, sent by God to prepare the way for the coming of the Messiah. The son of Elizabeth and Zechariah, a priest in the Temple, his birth had been prophesied to them in their old age; the name "John" was stated and so was the responsibility that he would carry on preparing the way for the Messiah. Elizabeth gave birth to her son six months before Mary, her cousin, gave birth to Jesus in Bethlehem.

Very little is known about his growing up except that he lived in the desert as one of the Nazirites. These were people of either sex who had taken a vow of separation and abstinence for some special form of service. (Samson was also a Nazirite.) It has also been suggested that John might have been one of the Essenes, a Jewish sect of monks (responsible for the Dead Sea Scrolls); there is no proof of this, however.

It will be necessary to explain the word "Messiah"—the anointed one, promised in the Old Testament to the Jews. (Israelites did not crown kings but anointed them with oil.) Christians recognize Jesus to be this person.

John is known as the Baptist because of his practice of baptizing; it was based on old Jewish customs.

AIM

1. To teach the story of this unusual and fearless man.
2. To show how his life was associated with Jesus, a cousin whom he rarely saw yet recognized to be the Messiah.

Lesson 1

INTRODUCTION

"Don't be afraid, Zechariah! God has heard your prayers, and your wife, Elizabeth, will bear you a son. How glad and happy you will be when he is born!" (Luke 1:14.) Before you tell the story, allow the children to imagine what sort of people the parents might be and suggest a few possible backgrounds.

SUGGESTED PROCEDURE

1. *An Unusual Birth* (Luke 1:5–25 and 57–66)

   Picture Zechariah, an old man performing his routine job of burning incense in the Temple. Outside, the people prayed . . . and waited . . . and wondered why he was spending such a long time inside (verse 21). Tell the parts of the story that you think applicable to your children's ages. The visit of the angel, the old man's dumbness and his sign language to an amazed people all lend themselves to graphic description—as do the family arguments about the baby's name and the eventual return of his voice!

   So John the Baptist was born.

2. *An Unusual Man with an Unusual Message* (Mark 1:1–6 and John 1:19–28)

We know little about his childhood but spend some time discussing how he lived when he left his parents and went into the desert. (Explain that there were many large desert or wilderness areas situated closely around the towns of Judea.)

He would have a very rugged appearance; as a Nazirite, his hair would never be cut and he wore camel hair and leather clothes. No fine food or wine for him—he ate wild honey and locusts! These may well have been the beans which were the fruit of the carob tree but they could also have been the insects commonly eaten by the very poor. (In some parts of the East, they still are.) One Bible Commentary states "Heads, wings and legs being removed, they are then boiled, stewed or roasted, dressed in butter and finally eaten—fresh, dried or salted". It may not be advisable to give this detailed recipe to every class!

Where would he live? We are not sure: perhaps a cave or a rough shelter; perhaps alone or with a few friends.

It seems that from an early age this unusual man knew that he had a very special job to do for God. Refer to the Old Testament verse from Isaiah quoted in Mark 1:2 and tell that John was this person. Remind the children that John was in his late twenties by then, and so was Jesus, of whom John was talking, but he was still living quietly as a carpenter in Nazareth. The people as yet knew nothing of him. His message to the people was:

(a) Get ready for the Lord. This would excite the Jews.

(b) Repent (turn away from your wrongdoing).

(c) Be baptized.

What a strange man and what a strange message! Discuss what baptism meant and describe the curiosity of the people as they crowded to the edge of the River Jordan to see what was happening.

OPTIONAL ACTIVITIES

1. Set up a Radio Jerusalem interview with the Baptist. Have the children think carefully through their introduction to the news and then record something similar to the conversation in John 1.

2. Build up a large zig-zag book, with pictures and writing mounted on stiff coloured paper. (This can also be used as a frieze but takes up less space.) There can be paintings of the Temple scene, the family arguments over the unsuspecting baby, the wild-looking young man in the desert, his preaching to the crowds and his baptisms in the river.

Lesson 2

INTRODUCTION

Read out "I baptize with water but among you stands the one you do not know. He is coming after me, but I am not good enough even to untie his sandals" (John 1:26).

John himself did not know it but the greatest moment of his life was very close. It happened the next day.

SUGGESTED PROCEDURE

John the Baptist could be portrayed under the following headings:

1. *A Prophet* (Mark 1:9–11, with reference to John 1:26–34).

   The beauty of this story is in its simplicity and it is best told in this way. Jesus came from Galilee to ask John to baptize him.

   Build up the picture of a crowd waiting on the banks of the river, some excited and happy, some curious and cynical, but all completely unaware that something was happening that was to have such a far-reaching effect on people throughout the centuries—for at the moment the "dove" descended, John realized that his cousin Jesus was the long-awaited Messiah. (God had promised this sign, John 1:33.) Finish with John's firm declaration, "I have seen it and I tell you that he is the Son of God". It was the culmination of his prophesying in the desert.

2. *A Teacher*

   What else did John do? He taught his disciples who followed him loyally, many becoming very concerned for him when Jesus, at the start of his ministry, gained more followers than he! In his later imprisonment they refused to abandon him and twenty years after he had died (Acts 19:3–4) people were still talking about him.

3. This section is not an essential part of the unit but may provoke interesting discussion amongst older pupils. Here some of John's teachings are merely listed:

   John 3:28–30. John uses the picture of himself as best man at a wedding happy to give the greater honour to the bridegroom. Emphasize the last verse—"He must become more important while I become less important".

   Luke 3:11. "Whoever has two shirts must give one to the man who has none and whoever has food must share it."

   Luke 3:12–13. "Some tax collectors came to be baptized and they asked him 'Teacher, what are we to do?' 'Don't collect more than is legal,' he told them."

Luke 3:14. "Some soldiers asked him, 'What about us? What are we to do?' He said to them, 'Don't take money from anyone by force or accuse anyone falsely. Be content with your pay'."

4. *A Martyr* (Luke 3:18–20; Mark 6:16–29)

One of John's bolder sayings led to his imprisonment and death. Herod the Great's son, Herod Antipas, was living with his brother's wife, Herodias, and the Baptist told him that this was a sin and against the law. For this John was arrested (who dare say such a thing to a "king"?) and shut up in a dreary fortress overlooking the Dead Sea.

Before you tell the story be sure that you have the rather gruesome details firmly in your mind. Allow the children first to talk about their knowledge of Eastern feasts and dancing and emphasize the contrast with the plain, rugged figure of the fearless man of God. (Was he fearless, or afraid but very brave?) It is a tragic story and the children should feel the very dramatic ending to a dramatic life.

Small wonder that Jesus said, "John is greater than any man who has ever lived" (Luke 7:28).

OPTIONAL ACTIVITIES

1. Complete the zig-zag book with more paintings and writing. Portray the three distinct parts of this lesson.
2. Discuss "courage" . . . fearless or afraid. Talk also about when to avoid trouble by keeping quiet and when to go headlong into risk by being frank.
3. Make a "Who's Who of Heroes"—other people anywhere or in any age who have died for their cause.

THE TEMPTATIONS OF JESUS

Matthew 4:1–11

AIM

To show that Jesus, though he was God, was also a man who had to struggle against the forces of evil and wrongdoing.
To show that because of this he understands how hard it can be for us.

INTRODUCTION

Refer to Jesus' boyhood and growing up (see the lesson on his visit to the Temple) and remind the children about the answer he gave to his mother about "having to be in his Father's house". Speak also about his baptism when he was about thirty (lesson on John the Baptist) and together read Mark 3:16–17. The dove, a sign of peace—was it God's seal of approval when Jesus was setting out to complete the task for which he had come to earth? And the voice—"This is my own dear son with whom I am pleased". What an encouragement! Talk a little about the awful doubts that must often have torn Jesus in two directions: death at the hands of his enemies or a "normal" family life in a carpenter's shop in Nazareth.

SUGGESTED PROCEDURE

Immediately after this wonderful experience, Jesus had to go away by himself into desert places to be alone and to think. The six weeks that followed were some of the hardest in his life. Ask the children if they know what an "anticlimax" is: to feel wonderful and then to come crashing down. Jesus may have experienced this—imagine what his thoughts may have been.

Have I merely imagined that God wants me to go through with this?

Shall I have the courage to stand in front of these people?

Why must I leave my home and my friends?

What if I fail?

Why me, Father?

Small wonder that he ate little over that time (verse 2). As with John, where did he live and what did he do all day? Build up a picture of the agonising longings and fears of this time which kept him from going back amongst people. We all need solitude sometimes to sort out lesser problems than this; it was as if Jesus was gathering strength to take the final step for God.

Children may well ask questions about the fact that Jesus was both God and man; although this concept can never be fully grasped by even the greatest thinkers, it may be possible to say to the children that the only way God could reach the people whom he loved so much was to become one of them. Then he would be able to show the extent of his love by his willingness to suffer the worst that anyone could imagine. The two sides of Jesus' nature must often have struggled in his mind, as now.

Jesus was tempted in three special ways.

(a) He was ravenously hungry! He knew that he would have the power to change the abundance of rocks strewn around into food—if he was "God's son". Notice the subtlety of that phrase (verse 3).

Jesus' answer was simply a reference from the Old Testament which he knew so well: "Man cannot live on bread alone but needs every word that God speaks". It is worth mentioning that Jesus never performed any miracle for his own comfort or safety.

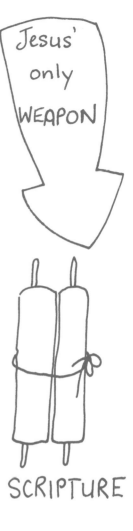

Jesus' only WEAPON

SCRIPTURE

HUNGER SUCCESS POWER

(b) "Go on; impress the people! Let them see with their own eyes how wonderful you are!" So came the second temptation where in imagination he was taken to the highest point in the temple. "A quick way to success", said the tempter "would be to jump from here into that deep, stony, valley below and let everyone see that you don't need to fall and die as an ordinary person would. **You** will be carried safely down—won't you?"

Again Jesus refused. How could he challenge his Father to protect him from the consequences of such a foolish action? He went this time to Deuteronomy 6:16 and said, "Do not put the Lord your God to the test".

(c) Lastly came a very wily temptation. In his imagination he was on the top of a high mountain. "Look around you", said the devil. What did Jesus see, we wonder? Rome and Athens, the seats of power and learning? Oceans with galleys and trading ships? Wealth and poverty? Palaces and prisons? Human need reaching into the distant lands of the whole world? In fact everyone whom God had sent him to save. "All this I will give you if you kneel down and worship me", went on the voice.

We cannot see to the depths of this terrible temptation but we do know that if Jesus had fallen at this moment, he could never have done what God wanted him to do—to win the hearts of men, women and children everywhere through God's love only and thus bring in the Kingdom of God on earth. Even though it meant his own death first, Jesus again said, "No!" Read verse 10. "Go away Satan. The scripture says, 'Worship the Lord your God and serve only him'."

This time the tempter knew that he was defeated and left Jesus alone, though John says in his Gospel that he did so, for a while only. Now angels came and provided food for Jesus. We do not know how this happened but Mark says that they also protected him from the wild animals that were around. It is good to think that perhaps he slept long and soundly after this ordeal!

OPTIONAL ACTIVITIES

Discuss with the class temptations that they have (lying, cheating, stealing, unkindness, etc.) and as a writing lesson have the children write out either 1 Corinthians 10:13 or Hebrews 4:15. (These are verses which speak about Jesus' sharing with us in all temptations and they assure us that he will never allow any test too great for us.)

These verses may be illustrated around the writing and mounted for the wall.

What do I do when I'm tempted?

God keeps his promise
1 Cor. 10:13

He was tempted in every way as we are
Heb. 4:15

JESUS' DISCIPLES

Matthews 4:18–22; Mark 1:16–20; Luke 5:1–11

INTRODUCTORY NOTE

Strictly speaking the disciples of Jesus, in the sense of those who followed his teachings, were many in number. The popular usage, however, "the disciples of Jesus" is usually taken to refer to the twelve apostles. They travelled with Jesus, observing him and learning from him. To these men, as first-hand witnesses, was entrusted the message which Jesus came to proclaim. This unit concentrates on those of the disciples about whom most is known (Lesson 5)—the fishermen (Lessons 1 to 3 and 6) and Matthew the tax-collector (Lesson 4).

By New Testament times there was a thriving fishing industry around the Sea of Galilee. Since this forms a considerable part of the background to the gospel story it would seem desirable to study in some depth the fishing scene in Israel in the time of Jesus.

There were two main types of fishing—fishing by seine net and fishing by cast net. In the former a net, perhaps several hundred metres long, would be let down from a boat and would hang vertically in the water. The fish were either encircled in deep water or dragged towards the shallow water. Two boats often worked in partnership. The cast net was circular with weights attached at intervals round the edge. Flung with a whirling motion by someone on the shore, it would land flat on the surface and as the weights sank it would be pulled ashore with the fish trapped inside. Rod and line were sometimes used and on occasion fish were speared.

Seine net fishing

barbel

lake sardines

cast net fishing

At approximately 200 metres below sea level, Galilee is the lowest freshwater lake in the world. It is 21 kilometres long and at its widest point it is almost 11 kilometres wide. Known also as the Lake of Gennesaret, or the Sea of Tiberias, it provided a means of livelihood for many people in the cities along its shores.

Fishing was generally done at night and the work was often dangerous because the lake is subject to fierce squalls which can arise almost without warning. On shore there was much to occupy the fishermen—mending and cleaning their nets, marketing and preserving fish and repairing boats and sails.

Some fish were eaten fresh while some were salted or dried and eaten with bread, as in the story of the loaves and fishes. Apart from two varieties, which have been introduced in recent times, the lake contains today the same kind of fish as in Jesus' time. It is reckoned that there are about twenty-five native species of which the most famous is the *Cichlid Tilapia*, better known as "St Peter's Fish".

Lesson 1   Fishermen in Galilee

AIM

To fill in some of the background to the gospel story.

INTRODUCTION

Show pictures relating to fishing in Lake Galilee in the past and in the present. Discuss similarities and differences between now and then and compare with the children's own experience of fishing.

SUGGESTED PROCEDURE

Spend some time building up a picture of the typical scenes Jesus would see as he walked by the Sea of Galilee. Points to include are:

(a) *Fishing by dragnet* Describe how it was done. If you have a length of net so much the better.
(b) *The catch* Describe the landing, sorting, marketing and use of fish.
(c) *Activities on shore* Elicit these—making, mending and cleaning nets, repairing boats and sails, etc.

OPTIONAL ACTIVITIES

1. Drama: This lesson gives ample opportunity for mime or dance-drama, in groups or as a class. The whole sequence could be portrayed and music used with it.
2. Build up an informative display:
    (a) Find out what kinds of fish are found in Lake Galilee. Each child should do as detailed a drawing as possible and label it for display.
    (b) In groups, or individually, children could find out all they can about different methods of fishing and illustrate them.
    (c) Find out ways of preserving fish and discuss.

3. Art: A few fish (fresh or smoked) should be brought to school and observed closely, then drawn accurately as for a scientific record. Another type of drawing or painting could then be done, using the fish as a stimulus but interpreting it artistically.

Lesson 2   Andrew and Peter; James and John

AIM

To introduce Andrew and Peter with their partners, James and John. To show how cast nets were used.

INTRODUCTION

Tell the children that Jesus had for several years stayed in Nazareth, his home town, helping his mother after Joseph had died but that now he was free to begin his main work of telling people about God and his plans for spreading the good news to all parts of the world. First of all he had to teach a small group thoroughly so that they would be able to carry on his work after his death which he knew would come after a few years.

He came to live by the shores of Galilee and gradually got to know the people around there.

SUGGESTED PROCEDURE

Tell about some fishermen friends Jesus recognized one day as he walked by the sea.

(a) *Andrew casting a net* Describe the net and how it was used.

(b) *Peter, Andrew's brother, mending a net* Discuss the scene. How might the net have become torn? Describe the cleaning and mending, and how some nets were lying on the rocks to dry, etc.

Jesus already knew these men (John 1:35–41). Andrew had heard John the Baptist's tribute to Jesus and had actually spent a night at his home. He had introduced Peter to Jesus.

(c) *James and John with their father, Zebedee* Further along Jesus recognized someone else—John, the friend who had been with Andrew on that occasion when they had first come to know one another. With his brother James (and their servants) he was helping their father, Zebedee. They were partners with Peter and Andrew in a fishing business, and were getting their nets ready.

FRIENDS OF JESUS

OPTIONAL ACTIVITIES

1. Craft: Try some netting. Find pictures of present-day fishermen mending their nets.
2. Music: The children may compose simple music depicting the sea in different moods.
3. Language: Write about the triumphs and disappointments of the fisherman's life. This could be linked to the music above.
4. Art: Silver or gold foil could be used to make a fish mobile.

Lesson 3   Call of the Disciples

AIM

To tell how Jesus asked these four men to leave their fishing business and go with him.

INTRODUCTION

Remind the children that they now know about four of Jesus' friends. These men knew Jesus personally and had heard his teaching. Some of them at least were convinced he was the long-awaited Messiah.

SUGGESTED PROCEDURE

Tell or read the story of the call of the disciples bringing out these points:
(a) Peter's boat to the rescue.
(b) An unexpected catch of fish.
(c) The call of the four and their response.

OPTIONAL ACTIVITIES

1. Discuss what Jesus meant by the words, "From now on you will be catching men". Do the children know of any "fishers of men" other than those mentioned in the Bible, e.g. missionaries, ministers, etc.?

2. Discussion: They all left a prosperous business. Why? What does this tell us of their attitude to Jesus? (They thought what he was doing was important; had learned a lot from him; thought he was the Messiah—the special messenger God had promised to send, etc.)
What does it tell us of Jesus' opinion of them? (diligent, hard-working, teachable, etc.).
3. Read: Psalm 107:23–31 "Some sailed over the ocean in ships . . . .".
This unit could form part of a project on the sea or on fishing.

Lesson 4   Matthew the Tax-collector

BACKGROUND NOTE

In 63 B.C. the Roman general Pompey occupied Jerusalem, and from then on Palestine was under the rule of Rome, as indeed was the whole Mediterranean world and beyond. It was during this time that Jesus was born under the reign of Augustus. He lived also during the reign of Tiberius (A.D 14–37) who was succeeded in turn by Claudius and Nero. For a time the puppet kings of the Herod family were allowed to retain some measure of authority. Later, Roman Governors were appointed, among them Pilate, Felix and Festus who figure in the Bible story.

As a rule, the Romans allowed subject nations to pursue their own religion and customs, which explains, for example, why Pilate was eager to wash his hands of the whole affair when the Jews insisted on the crucifixion.

The Roman Empire brought certain advantages—good roads and buildings, for instance. To pay for these and for the upkeep of an army of occupation they levied taxes, the collectors being local volunteers who usually earnéd thereby the contempt and hatred of their fellow-countrymen. Two tax-collectors whose lives were influenced by Jesus were Matthew and Zacchaeus.

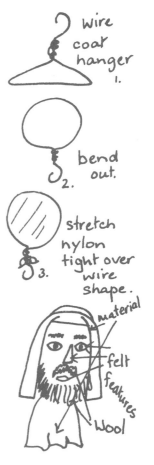

Among Romans who figure in the New Testament are a centurion of the garrison in Capernaum (Luke 7) and Cornelius, a captain in the "Italian Regiment" in Caesarea (Acts 10 and 11).

Since the Roman occupation is part of the New Testament background it is worth taking time, at some point, to study it in greater detail. Relevant topics perhaps for project work might be:

Roads and buildings;
System of government;
The army;
Money, taxes;
Laws;
Roman gods and religion generally.

Matthew 9:9–13; Luke 5:27–31

AIM

To show something of the background to the gospel story. To introduce Matthew who became a disciple of Jesus.

INTRODUCTION

This could be an opportunity to do some work on the Romans in Palestine. If this is not desired, find out what the children already know about the Romans. Point out that at the same time as the Romans were in Britain they were masters of Israel also. The powerful Romans knew nothing of Jesus. They worshipped their own gods—Mars, Vulcan, Jupiter, etc.—all unaware of the baby born in Bethlehem. They tolerated other religions which was why Jesus was free to choose disciples whom he would teach about the kingdom of God.

SUGGESTED PROCEDURE

Go on to tell the story of Matthew:

1. *Tax-collectors* Tell about the need for them and how they were disliked as they often took more than their due.
2. *Matthew's call* Tell about his work and the insults he would suffer. Probably he often saw Jesus and listened to his teaching and when Jesus actually asked him, a social outcast, to become a follower he gave up everything to do so. He would be poorer—but happier.
3. *His farewell party* Note the contrast between the attitude of the Pharisees and that of Jesus and discuss. Jesus befriended the despised one and took him into the company of his close friends. (Much later Matthew wrote the story of Jesus' life.)

OPTIONAL ACTIVITIES

1. Project work on the Romans as suggested in the background note.
2. Find out the effect Jesus had on the life of another tax-collector, Zacchaeus.
3. Talk about today's social outcasts—and why it is that some groups despise others. Do they have a point? In what ways are we all equal in God's sight?

Lesson 5   The Appointment of the Twelve

Mark 3:13–19; Matthew 10:1–4; Luke 6:12–16

AIM

To establish the fact that Jesus had twelve disciples, or apostles, and to consider their role.

INTRODUCTION

Recapitulate briefly the invitation given to the four fishermen and Matthew to leave their work and accompany Jesus.

SUGGESTED PROCEDURE

Tell about the call of the twelve:

1. *Jesus' strategy for extending God's Kingdom*
   Explain that the word "disciple" means a pupil, a learner, and that it is applied in a wide sense to those who were eager to understand and follow the teachings of a recognized authority—in this case, Jesus. In that sense Jesus had many disciples. But he wanted a smaller band whom he would teach in more detail and who after his death would be witnesses, proclaiming what they knew from first-hand experience. The choosing of that group was to have far-reaching consequences. Let the children find out what Jesus did before calling them. (He prayed all night—Luke 6:12.)

2. *Jesus chooses the twelve*
   Let the children read Mark 3:13–19 or make copies of it for them, then ask the following questions. (For some classes they might be too easy.)
   (a) How many disciples did Jesus call?
   (b) What special name did he give them?
   (c) Write their names.
   (d) What nickname did Jesus give to James and John, the fishermen?
   (e) Can you think how they might have earned this nickname? (We are not told but there's no harm in having a guess.)

(f)   Which of the disciples did Scotland adopt as its patron saint?

(g)   Where did all this take place?

(h)   What were the apostles chosen to do?

You may use these questions and their answers as a basis for discussion. The following information might be useful.

"Apostle" means "sent one". They were to be sent out by Jesus both during his lifetime and after his death to help in the extension of his work.

Peter, James and John became his closest friends. James and John were brothers. Peter and Andrew were brothers.

John wrote a gospel, the three letters that bear his name and the Book of Revelation.

Bartholomew is thought to be the Nathaniel of John 1:43–51.

Thomas was a twin and known as "doubting Thomas"—the reason is told in John 20:26–29.

Simon "the zealot" may have belonged to the nationalist group known as "The Zealots" who rebelled against the Romans in A.D. 6 and again in A.D. 65–70.

James was put to death by Herod Agrippa I, a few years after Jesus' death.

For Judas' betrayal see Matthew 26:14–16 and 47–56, and 27:3–9. For further insight into his character see John 12:4–6.

3.   *Their mission* Luke 9:1–7

Was to preach, to heal, to cast out demons. Their powers, derived from Jesus, were parallell to his and were given to authenticate their message.

4.   *Their final commission* Matthew 28:16–19

"Go, then, to all people everywhere (not the Jews only)

And make them my disciples;

Baptize them . . .

Teach them to obey . . ."

Then comes Jesus' pledge: "And I will be with you always".

OPTIONAL ACTIVITIES
1. Read Mark's gospel which is thought by many to have been written down by him from accounts of Jesus' life told him by Peter. It is the shortest gospel and older children can quite easily read it through for themselves.
2. To find out how the apostles carried out their commission after Jesus' death, children need look no further than the Acts of the Apostles. More demanding than Mark, it should yet be within the grasp of the brighter pupils.

Lesson 6   Peter

BACKGROUND NOTE
Peter is an apostle about whom quite a lot is known. Impulsive, perceptive, enthusiastic, at times over-confident, by turns cowardly and courageous, he comes over as a very human person far removed from the plaster-saint image that the word "apostle" perhaps conjures up for some. His mission was primarily to the Gentiles (i.e. non-Jewish peoples). Two of his letters form part of the New Testament. There is a belief that, like his master, he died on a cross.

AIM
To tell in outline the story of Peter's life. To show how being a disciple of Jesus worked out in practice.

INTRODUCTION
Here are quotations by a Biblical character. Can the children identify him? Here they are in the order in which they were spoken. Guess who.
(a) "Go away from me, Lord! I am a sinful man!" (Luke 5:8).
(b) "You are the Messiah, the Son of the living God." (Matthew 16:16).
(c) "I will never leave you (i.e. Jesus), even though all the rest do!" (Matthew 26:33).
(d) "Woman, I don't even know him! (i.e. Jesus)." (Luke 22:57).
(e) "Lord, you know everything; you know that I love you!" (John 21:17).
Further clues:
He was a fisherman, an apostle, and had a brother called Andrew.

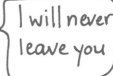

SUGGESTED PROCEUDRE
Tell the story of Peter or read and discuss the relevant excerpts.

1. *Peter the Fisherman*
Describe his life, sketching in the background as in the introductory note about fishing. It was his brother Andrew who originally introduced him to Jesus (John 1:35–42).
He belonged to the lakeside town of Bethsaida but may have moved to Capernaum. He was married and his wife's mother was staying with them either permanently or for a visit. Tell the story of how she was

cured of a "high fever" by Jesus one Sabbath day when he and some others were invited to Peter's home after attending worship at the synagogue in Capernaum. (Mark 1:29–31; Luke 4:38, 39).

2. *Peter the disciple*
Tell about Jesus' invitation to join him in his work (Luke 5:1–11) and, later, Jesus' choice of him to be an apostle (Luke 6:12–16). Luke 9:1–6 describes his life as an apostle.

3. *Peter fails a test* (Luke 22:31–34 and 54–62)
Peter had failed both himself and Jesus. He had been cowardly and untruthful after being proud and over-confident. Talk with the children about Peter's failure. Why did he say that he didn't know Jesus? How did he feel when he realized what he'd done? What does that tell us about Peter's attitude to Jesus? What might his thoughts have been about himself? About his future?
Talk about the children's experiences of letting themselves and others down—if the discussion develops spontaneously. They may like to write about such an occasion, perhaps only for themselves, not necessarily handing in their writing.

4. *Peter restored* (John 21)
Peter thought he had ruined his life and particularly his relationship with Jesus. Can the class guess what he decided to do? Go back to his fishing! So off he went to Lake Galilee and six of the others went with him. John 21 tells what happened. Verse 7—"the disciple whom Jesus loved" is thought to be John. There are hints in the gospels that Jesus was particularly friendly with him.
Why, do they think, did Jesus ask the question of Peter three times? (Perhaps because of Peter's denial three times that he knew Jesus, he gave Peter the opportunity to cancel out these denials with three declarations of love and loyalty.) "Follow me" (verse 19) said Jesus and Peter was back on the old footing, restored. (Compare with people refreshed by rest and nourishment.) Peter had learned valuable lessons.

Can the children think of any? (Failing is not the end: it's possible to make a new beginning: you can learn from failure: it's not good to boast or think yourself better than others: he should have asked God to give him courage: Jesus doesn't dismiss people when they fail but cares for them (see 1 Peter 5:7).)

John 21:19—Peter died bravely and unselfishly.

OPTIONAL ACTIVITIES

These may be used at appropriate points in the narrative.

1. Read an example of the kind of message Peter gave to his listeners in Acts 10:34–43.

2. Read about one of the adventures he had in Acts 12:1–19.

3. Find out: If you go to a restaurant in Galilee today, on the menu you may find "St Peter's fish". Find out all you can about it, draw it and read about the incident that lies behind its name (Matthew 17:24–27). Of course we don't know that it actually was this species in which the coin was found—but it has a big mouth!

4. Writing: Put yourself in Peter's shoes and tell his own story. Possible starting points: "Fishing's been my life," or "Memories of Jesus" (Mark's gospel is thought to be based on Peter's reminiscences). Alternatively, write a poem giving his thoughts after denying Jesus, or write prose or poetry on "My Friend Peter" as if by one of the other disciples.

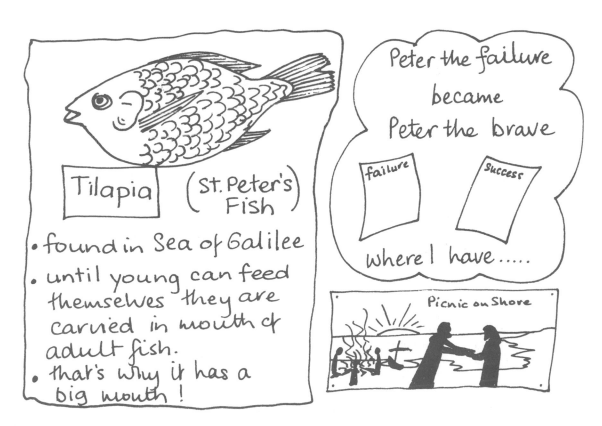

Tilapia (St. Peter's) Fish

- found in Sea of Galilee
- until young can feed themselves they are carried in mouth of adult fish.
- that's why it has a big mouth!

Peter the failure became Peter the brave

failure

Success

where I have .....

Picnic on Shore

MARTHA, MARY AND LAZARUS

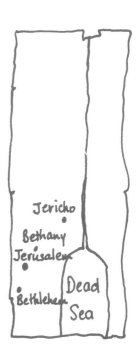

Luke 10:38–41

AIM

1. To show Jesus in an ordinary home setting and incidentally teach about homes in New Testament Israel.
2. To show the contrasting personalities of two sisters and how both could serve Jesus.

INTRODUCTION

Do some work on differences in personal traits. This could include graphs and diagrams showing height, eye colour, preferences (colour, food, etc.), activities (cricket, piano-playing, etc.), "Guess who?" games, studies in literature, etc. Bring out the point that each has strengths, perhaps weaknesses too. No one personality type should be considered better or worse than another.

SUGGESTED PROCEDURE

1. Tell about the home in Bethany (meaning incidentally "house of dates") about 3 km from Jerusalem on the far side of the Mount of Olives. When visiting Jerusalem, at that time a large city with a population of perhaps a quarter of a million, Jesus was glad to stay with his friends in Bethany. If Martha's home was one of the more wealthy ones it would be built Roman-style round a courtyard.

   The people who lived there (whether in the same house or in separate homes is not clear) were Mary, Martha and their brother Lazarus.

2. Read (or have duplicated copies) from Luke 10:38–41 and have the children write down their impressions of what Mary and Martha were like, e.g.

   Martha: busy, up and doing, wanting everything to be nice for Jesus, anxious, hospitable. Perhaps it was her home, etc.

   Mary: quiet, listening and learning, dreamy, not so practical, more thoughtful.

3. Discuss Jesus' reply. Did he say one person was preferable to another? Did he say one attitude was preferable to another? What if Martha also had sat down to listen to Jesus' teaching?

OPTIONAL ACTIVITIES

1. Discuss, or write about, priorities. What do the children think are the important things?

   Children's actions reflect their choice as a rule—the choosing is therefore largely unconscious. It is only as we get older that we become more conscious of the element of choice.

2. Sing: "I listen and I listen" (*Come and Praise*).

STORIES JESUS TOLD

Lesson 1   The Lost Son

Luke 15:11–27

AIM

To tell the story of the Lost Son and to help children understand that as a loving father God will forgive us when we ask him.

INTRODUCTION

Explain that Jesus even cared for the dishonest tax collectors of his time. The Jewish religious leaders complained, so Jesus told this story (called a parable) to show that these were some of the people who needed him most.

SUGGESTED PROCEDURE

1. Sketch in the background of a wealthy home and a happy family life. Describe how when the younger of the two sons grew up, he wished that he could leave home, see a bit of the world and enjoy life. As the idea grows in his mind, he decides to ask his father for the money he would be leaving him in his will. It would not be much fun going to see the big wide world without lots of money to spend! His father agrees. (This could lead to discussion.)
2. Describe the excitement and anticipation of the son as he packs and leaves home with high hopes. Talk about ways in which he would spend his money—parties, treating friends, etc., —until one day he realizes that his money is all gone.
3. To make matters worse there is a famine. He is hungry and cold, has lost all his friends (why?), and is probably lonely and a bit afraid. He begins to look for a job and persuades a farmer to let him feed the pigs.

Make up Cartoon Series of the Son's adventures.

- Take a set of slides of the story.
- Dress up as characters either in Biblical Times or To-day's.
- Write script then tape it and play it as you show slides.
- Everyone can join in project.

4. As he watches them eating he even envies them and wishes he could have some of their food—but alas, no one gives him anything. What would his thoughts be? Would he remember his lovely comfortable home and feel sorry? Would he wonder if he dare go home again?

5. Gradually the thought becomes a hope, and then a resolution. He is starving, while his father's servants have enough to eat. He decides to go back and say that he is sorry, not only that he has sinned against his father but also against God; he does not deserve to be treated as a son any more but would be happy to be a servant.

6. Vividly describe the journey home—apprehension—father running towards him—tremendous welcome—speech cut short—instead of slinking in he is treated as an honoured guest and is given a tremendous party. Describe the change in him. Ask the children in what ways God is like that father.

OPTIONAL ACTIVITIES

1. One pupil could read the story from the Bible, while others mime it.
2. Comic strip pictures could be drawn by various groups and fitted together to form a whole, which is then displayed.
3. Write a version of this story set in modern times (narrative or play).

Lesson 2   The Sower

Matthew 13:1–9 and 18–23

AIM

To relate this parable and to help the children understand, even in some small measure, something of its meaning.

INTRODUCTION

Everywhere he went, crowds followed Jesus to hear what he would say. Tell how one day he went to the sea shore and, because there were so many people, he got into a boat and spoke to them as they listened on the beach.

SUGGESTED PROCEDURE

1. By demonstration or illustration, show how a farmer in those days would sow his seed by hand. Describe what happens to the seed mentioned in the story.

seed fell

(a) Some falls beside a path and the birds come and eat it.

(b) Some seed lands on soil too rocky for strong roots. Plants spring up but are scorched and withered by the sun.

(c) Others fall among thorn bushes but the plants are choked and soon die because there is not enough room.

(d) Some fall on good soil and produce a harvest of corn, thirty, sixty and one hundred times what he had planted.

2. Jesus explained the parable like this:

(a) The hard path is like the heart of a person who hears God's good news, but does not understand it. That person is careless and pays little attention. The Evil One snatches the seed away and what was heard is forgotten.

(b) The rocky soil describes a person who listens to the words of Jesus and seems enthusiastic. When things get hard (e.g. trouble comes or people laugh at him) he just gives up.

(c) The thorny soil is like the person who hears, believes and wants to follow Jesus. Other things however, like love of money, take all his attention and there is less and less room for God in his life.

(d) The good soil stands for those who hear God's word, believe it and go on to live for Jesus. They will help others to love him too.

3. Perhaps to older pupils it could be explained that the seed is the Word of God, the sower is God (using people like teachers, preachers, writers, missionaries, etc.) while the soil is the heart/mind/understanding of a person.

OPTIONAL ACTIVITIES

1. Story could be illustrated by drawing four separate pictures, with captions below. A large sower could accompany them.

2. As an added interest discuss present-day people whose lives have been changed, taking an extract from a missionary book or making reference to a well-known Christian pop-star, television personality, tennis player, etc.

3. This could be part of a wider project on farming.

Lesson 3   The Mustard Seed

Matthew 13:31–32

AIM

To show by comparison with something very familiar how God's kingdom begins in the hearts of people, and that when they love him and want to follow him, others may be helped.

INTRODUCTION

Talk about planting seeds. Children could be encouraged to plant their own, or bring to school and observe the growth of one already planted. Pictures could be shown of various trees and plants, and seeds collected. Stress the size and strength of a tree in comparison with its beginning as a tiny seed.

SUGGESTED PROCEDURE

1. Explain that when people learn about Jesus, and want to love and please him, he becomes the king of their lives. It could be pointed out that there are people in his kingdom all over the world, speaking different languages, and belonging to different nations. That kingdom begins in a small way with each individual person and keeps growing.
2. As Jesus went about doing good, loving and helping people, so his followers want to do the same.

OPTIONAL ACTIVITIES

Depending upon the age and stage of the children, there could be discussion of the many ways in which Christians have helped and cared for others—educationally, socially, medically, as well as spiritually, e.g. Elizabeth Fry, David Livingstone, Shaftesbury, Martin Luther King, Mother Teresa, Gladys Aylward, Corrie Ten Boom.

NOTE: The parable of the yeast would have the same meaning.

Lesson 4   The Hidden Treasure and the Pearl

Matthew 13:44–45

AIM

To tell about two people who were willing to give up everything to find Jesus.

INTRODUCTION

Talk about the things that are most important to the children. To what lengths would they go to obtain them? Discuss what that might mean for various members of the family—saving, sacrifice, being in earnest, not giving up, etc.

SUGGESTED PROCEDURE

1. Describe how a man discovers hidden treasure in a field. What might it be? What are his feelings?—excitement, happiness? He carefully hides it, sells all that he has and saves up his money until he has enough to buy the field. But what comes with the field?—the treasure. Nothing else seems to matter to him.
2. A merchant, who buys and sells precious stones, comes across a pearl that he knows is a very special one, of very great value. He is determined to have it, so what does he do? He sells everything in order to buy it. Think of the things he would have to do without! That did not seem to matter to him at all.
3. Meaning—The Bible calls the truth about Jesus "treasure". It is fairly easy for us in this country to have a Bible but sometimes we don't bother to read it. With older children there could be comparison with people in other countries and the lengths to which they would go to have a Bible to learn about God. Suggest ways in which we could find the treasure.

OPTIONAL ACTIVITIES

1. To help to find our way about the Bible, have quizzes and "find the book in the Bible" competition.
2. A book could be read aloud, such as *Mary Jones and her Bible*.
3. Some research could be done with older children into how our Bible came to us. Reference could also be made to the ongoing work of translation for jungle tribes, etc. The National Bible Society will give information and has an excellent display for anyone who can visit it in London.

Lesson 5   The Two House-builders

Matthew 7:24–26

AIM

To tell the story of two men whose choices had contrasting effects on their lives.

INTRODUCTION

Children are familiar with building sites, concrete mixers, etc. Talk about housebuilding and ask what the workmen must do before they begin to build the walls. Elicit from the children that the most important part would be the laying of the foundations. What would happen if these were not strong? Cracks would appear in the walls and eventually the house would fall.

SUGGESTED PROCEDURE

1. Tell the story of the man who decided to build a house. Details could be mentioned such as site, view, etc., but most important of all, he built it on a rock, making sure that it had a strong foundation. Describe graphically the storm, rain, wind and rivers overflowing. What happened to this man's house? It stood firm, because it was built on a rock.

2. In contrast, another man built a house. He too thought of the position and wanted a lovely view of the sea. Having found what he thought was the ideal spot, he began to build on the sand. The sea was calm and the sun was shining. You can guess what happened! When the rain poured down, the winds blew, and rivers overflowed, what happened to his house? It crumbled to the ground.

3. Which man was the wiser? Jesus had many things to teach people while he was on earth. Those who listen and obey his words are, he said, like the wise man who built his house upon the rock. What about those who pay no attention and go their own way? Jesus said they are like the foolish man who built his house upon the sand. An elaboration of the meaning may be possible in the upper classes of the primary school, where children could go from the abstract to actual examples. There could be some discussion about the consequences of the choices we make for our lives.

OPTIONAL ACTIVITIES

1. Art: Contrast two houses in a storm—as each is affected, with captions added.

2. Environmental Studies: Visit a local building site. If possible children could study plans, depth of foundation in relation to height, etc. Photographs could be taken and a workbook could be compiled later.
3. Sing: "The wise man built his house upon the rock" *(C.S.S.M. Choruses)* or "Everybody's Building" *(Come and Praise)*.

Lesson 6   The Pharisee and the Tax-collector

Luke 18:9–14

AIM

To help the children to have a right attitude when they pray to God.

INTRODUCTION

Pharisees were members of a strict religious group. One particular Pharisee claimed that he tried to keep all God's laws, and many others that had been added over the years. He was proud of this and looked down on other people. Although he went regularly to the Temple, there was often little love for God in his heart and he could be selfish and unforgiving. But he thought he was all right. Generally, although not loved, he would be respected by others.

On the other hand a tax-collector was hated—a social outcast. There were two main reasons for this:

1. He was employed by the Romans, who had conquered the Jews, to raise money for the occupation of their land.
2. There was no fairness in the system. The tax-collector demanded that far more money be paid in taxes than was necessary. Much of this he put in his own pocket and so became rich. He was dishonest and greedy.

SUGGESTED PROCEDURE

1. Ask why people go to church, eliciting the answers—to worship God, to sing to him, to pray, etc. Explain that in Jesus' day every Jew would go regularly to the Temple. Not all were sincere, and as Jesus watched them he knew how they were feeling in their hearts and what their motives were. He told this story:
2. One day two men happened to go to the Temple to pray at the same time. One was a Pharisee and the other a tax-collector. We can imagine the attitude of the Pharisee. He would dress in his best clothes, walk proudly along hoping everyone would see him, and march in, taking up a position well away from the other man.
3. He did not really pray, but boasted to God about what a good person he was. (With older children the content of his prayer could be discussed more fully.) To make things worse he told God how much better he considered himself to be than the tax-collector. How differently the tax-collector behaved. Going into the Temple quietly, he stood all by himself and hung his head in shame. Beating himself with his hands, he cried to God to have pity on him because of his sinfulness.

A phylactery
—slightly smaller

2 Matchboxes

longblack
shoe lace

• Glue lace
between 2
match boxes.
• Paint black.

• Worn on
forehead
• insert some
Hebrew script
inside boxes—
the Law.

Prayer
Shawl

• white cotton
material.
• stripes with
blackfelt pen
• tassels of
black wool.

4. What did Jesus think of these two men and the way in which they prayed? "The tax-collector," said Jesus, "was in the right with God when he went home." He was humble, and sorry, so God would bless him, whereas the Pharisee was so full of pride that he needed to be humbled.

OPTIONAL ACTIVITIES

1. Discuss attitudes of people today compared with those of the Pharisees— are there similarities?
2. Children could be encouraged to write out their own prayers with emphasis on God's holiness, greatness, loving kindness and willingness to forgive.
3. Younger children might like to draw the two men at prayer.

4. Suggested hymns from *The Church Hymnary*: "Lord Jesus, be thou with us now, As in thy house in prayer we bow;" "Jesus Christ, I look to thee"; "Holy Spirit, hear us."

Lesson 7   The Talents

Matthew 25:14–30

AIM

To help children to see that God has given each one talents, and to encourage the development of these.

INTRODUCTION

A "talent" is variously interpreted in different translations. It apparently was a large sum of money. The number of "talents" or "coins" was fairly distributed according to each man's ability, so that no one in the story had an unfair advantage or responsibility. As a detailed explanation would be a difficult concept for children to grasp, it could be simply explained to them as ability, or opportunities, which each of us has been given to a greater or lesser degree.

SUGGESTED PROCEDURE

1. *Responsibility*

   A man who owned a business had to go on a journey, so he called three men who worked for him and distributed money, trusting them to use it wisely and well. Describe how it was shared out and discuss with the children what he expected each one to do—work hard, be honest, use his abilities to the full, make profits, etc.

2. *Reaction*

   Two of the men wanted to do their best for their employer and to make a success of his business. Imagine how pleased they were when he came home and they were able to tell him that both of them had doubled the amount given to him at the beginning. What about the third man? He began to make excuses for having done nothing and even blamed his employer, telling lies about him. "I was afraid," he said, "and buried the money."

3. *Result*

   How pleased the employer was with the two men who had done so well—not only because the business was thriving, but also because they had been so faithful. He praised them, gave them promotion, and they were able to share his happiness. How different it was for the third man! He was told he was lazy and bad. Why hadn't he just put the money in the bank where it would have gained interest? His share of the money was taken from him and he was sent away. He missed all the happiness that the others enjoyed.

4. *Application*

   Ask what the children think mattered more: how much was given or what each one did with what he had. God has given all of us particular gifts or talents. Children could suggest what these might be (in a general sense). Stress that if we do not use and develop them we fail in living useful lives, helping others, etc.—and so miss out on much happiness.

OPTIONAL ACTIVITIES

1. Ask the children to write down any talent or gift they have and say how they can improve or develop it. How could they use this talent when they are grown up?
2. Write out and illustrate: "Work hard at whatever you do" (Ecclesiastes 9:10).
3. Suggested hymns from the Church Hymnary: "The wise may bring their learning"; "Just as I am, thine own to be".
4. Prayer: Lord Jesus, thank you for giving us the ability to do so much in this world. Help us not to be lazy, but always to do our best. Amen.

PEOPLE JESUS HELPED

Lesson 1 The Man with the Paralyzed Hand

Matthew 12:9–14; (also Mark 3:1–6; Luke 6:6–11)

BACKGROUND NOTE

The Jewish Sabbath, the seventh day of the week, begins on Fridays at sunset. It is regarded as a day of rest and refreshment, and for worship at synagogue and at home. It is a day set aside from weekday work and interests. During the three hundred years before the time of Jesus many stringent regulations were introduced and enforced for Sabbath-keeping, which made it burdensome. Jesus by his actions and words challenged these additions and aroused opposition from the Jewish leaders.

AIM

To tell how Jesus healed a man, and tell what were his priorities and standards in spite of opposition.

INTRODUCTION

Ask the pupils what makes Sunday different, and discuss reasons why it is good to have such a day. Introduce the Jewish Sabbath, with its origins in the creation story (Genesis 2:1–3) and in the Commandments (Exodus 20:8–11), pointing out that it is still observed by Jews today. It may be useful to say that the early Christians made Sunday, the first day of the week, their day of worship in memory of the Resurrection on that day.

SUGGESTED PROCEDURE

1. Describe a typical synagogue service, with the women and children in a gallery or other place set apart, and the men, with heads covered, sitting around the central reading desk. There would be prayer, readings from the scriptures by men from the congregation and then teaching by an invited layman, followed by discussion.

Visit to a Synagogue

Visit your local church

I pray 3 times 9am 12noon 3pm I worship in the synagogue

The Service is on the Sabbath and consists of... Reading Prayer discussion

I go to Church on Sundays

I sit with the Children in a different part of synagogue

What I do on Sundays

WHAT'S ON IN CHURCH...

2. It would be after Jesus had been teaching that the test question came, from those who were there only to catch him out. We can imagine the silence that fell as they waited for his answer.

3. Jesus drew their attention to the fact that emergencies could be dealt with, within the Sabbath regulations—but this case was not an emergency. Then he challenged them to acknowledge that it was better to help someone on the Sabbath than to harm them. This must have struck home for they were seeking to harm him. He then proceeded to heal the man, thus openly breaking the law. In Luke 6:6 we are told that it was the man's right hand that was paralyzed. Jesus had seen the man's need and met it, restoring his ability to earn his living.

OPTIONAL ACTIVITIES

1. Make a model of a scripture scroll as used in a synagogue.
2. Discuss what should be our criteria for deciding what to do or not to do on Sundays. This is a situation that demands tact and discretion but it is valuable to think out our reasons and motives.

Lesson 2   At the Pool of Bethesda

John 5:1–9

AIM

To tell how Jesus healed a cripple and note what that involved for the man.

INTRODUCTION

Ask the children to remember times when they were ill and had to stay in bed for some days feeling unwell. Draw out comments on how their lives were different then with meals in bed, gifts and extra attention. Ask next how they felt when nearly back to full health. Did they regret the ending of this time of being the centre of attention—that they would have to go back to normal responsibilities—and school?

SUGGESTED PROCEDURE

1. Describe Jerusalem, crowded for one of the religious festivals with people everywhere, including around the Pool of Bethesda (or Bethzatha) in the north-east of the city. The pool was obviously a well-known place for invalids, because of the belief in the healing properties of the water when it bubbled up, as it did occasionally.

2. Among the many sick people was a man who had been ill for thirty-eight years, obviously unable to walk, and who was alone. Discuss what his life must have been like up to that time, possibly as a beggar.

3. Tell how Jesus made his way through the crowd and approached the man. Jesus' question, "Do you want to get well?" was not as simple as it seemed. With the years, he might have become despairing, resigned and so accustomed to his way of life that any thought of change would be alarming. His reply showed a determination and patient persistence which meant that he did wish for healing.

4. Jesus' command, "Get up" was asking the man to attempt the impossible, but he was willing to obey, and as he moved he found that he was now able to rise. His health was restored! Bring out the drama of the situation.

5. He was commanded to pick up his mat and walk. In this way Jesus set him out on his new life, vastly different from that of the past, a life of new opportunities and responsibilities.

OPTIONAL ACTIVITIES

1. Accounts of the happenings of that day could be written
   (a) as a diary kept by the man who was healed, or
   (b) as a letter to a friend or relative living far from Jerusalem.
2. A class frieze could be made, perhaps with collage, of the pool, showing the five arches, the water bubbling up and the crowds of people including many invalids.

Lesson 3   The Man with Four Friends

Mark 2:1-12 (also Matthew 9:1–8; Luke 5:17–26)

AIM

To tell how four men cared enough to bring their friend to Jesus.

INTRODUCTION

Ask the children to recall situations when they have been in a hurry, and have been hindered by crowds of people. It could be in a large shop, a busy street or a crowded playground or bus. Discuss the reasons for hurrying, whether personal or to help someone else, and how they felt when delayed by the crowd. Did they persist or give up trying?

SUGGESTED PROCEDURE

1. Jesus had by this time become well known as a healer and a teacher and people gathered wherever he went. According to custom, the door would be standing hospitably open and the people soon filled the house. Many more crowded round the door, no doubt blocking the narrow street as they listened to Jesus teaching.

105

2. Describe the arrival of the four men, carrying the light stretcher bed or mat on which lay their paralyzed friend, and their resourcefulness in overcoming the obstacle of the crowds. The house would have a flat roof and an outside stair. The wood and tiles of the roof would be easily removed and simple to replace. Tell of the surprise and interest caused by the man being lowered into the room.

3. Today we know that illness is sometimes caused by mental attitudes, but for the Jews at that time all illness was caused by sin. It may be that the man, believing this, was in despair and so had no expectation of a cure. His friends' faith and determination impressed Jesus. His first words dealt with the man's feelings of guilt and despair. They also caused a sensation among his hearers, for forgiveness of sin was the prerogative of God alone.

4. Knowing this, Jesus openly challenged his critics by commanding the man to get up, thus proving his power to forgive as well as heal, and bringing peace for the man's mind as well as new health for his body. The reaction of the spectators was (a) amazement, (b) acknowledgment that they had seen the power of God at work.

OPTIONAL ACTIVITIES

1. The class will enjoy dramatizing this incident.
2. This lesson could lead on to a study of the emergency services of today, and how the children should react when involved themselves. There are many ways that we can care for others.

Lesson 4   The Centurion's Servant

Luke 7:1–10 (also Matthew 8:5–13)

BACKGROUND NOTE

The children may know of centurions from studies of the Romans. A centurion was roughly the equivalent of a sergeant-major and was an important person in the Roman army, in charge of about a hundred men. Slaves at that time belonged entirely to their master who could do what he wished with them.

AIM

To show how the character and personality of the centurion enabled Jesus to heal the slave.

INTRODUCTION

Discuss with the children the purpose of rules and laws in society, especially where it affects them: at home, in school and on the roads. Do they like to be told what to do? Are there times when they tell someone else what to do? Show that we all have times to obey and to command. Mention could be made of the position of slaves in Roman times.

SUGGESTED PROCEDURE

1. Palestine at the time of Jesus was occupied and ruled by the Romans, and at the town of Capernaum there was a Roman garrison with a centurion in charge. He must have been drawn to the worship of the Jewish God, because he built a synagogue. In his household he had slaves, one of whom was ill and most surprisingly he was concerned. Normally no one would bother about a slave who was ill but this centurion cared about those in his charge.
2. Tell how he approached the elders of the local synagogue asking them to speak to Jesus on his behalf, seeking healing for his slave.

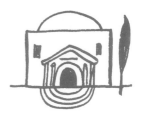

3. As Jesus set out for the centurion's home the crowd would have been aware that it was against their law to enter a Gentile house. It says much for the centurion's humility that he sent another delegation to avoid this.

4. The message he sent implied so much. From his own experience he knew what it was to obey and to command. Therefore he reasoned that Jesus, with his divine authority, would be able merely to give the order for his slave to get well. No wonder Jesus marvelled. The slave was healed without Jesus going to his bedside. The centurion's faith had revealed to men more of the power of God.

OPTIONAL ACTIVITIES

1. Make a frieze called "What can I do to help?" Have pictures with captions for the centurion
   (a) caring for his slave who was ill;
   (b) helping the Jews by building a synagogue.
   The children might also draw and write captions showing ways in which they can help others.

2. Groups can find out about slavery in the ancient world, in America and elsewhere, and about its abolition.

3. Discuss the importance of keeping rules and laws, and draw up a list of new ideas for laws which would help the society the children live in.

Lesson 5　　The Ten Lepers

Luke 17:11–19

AIM

To tell how Jesus willingly healed the lepers, and how they responded.

INTRODUCTION

Discuss with the children their feelings on new situations, such as going to a new school, or joining a club where they know no one. Lead on to the subject of unpopularity, of being left out of things and the unhappiness this causes.

SUGGESTED PROCEDURE

1. Find out what they know about leprosy, and explain that it was incurable in Jesus' time. There was such fear of leprosy that those who contracted it had to leave home to live in isolation, poverty and misery as the disease took its course. Lack of sensation caused sores and ulcers to develop leading to the loss of fingers, toes, hands and feet.

2. Introduce the group of men. They would have come from different villages, trades and backgrounds. In fact at least one of them was a Samaritan. Jews regarded Samaritans as outsiders, as their Jewish ancestors had intermarried with other peoples. Their common plight had drawn them together. Somehow they had heard of Jesus, and how he had healed many people who had come to him.

3. Imagine how they felt when they found that Jesus was nearby, their feelings of hope and desperation. This was their chance, perhaps their only chance, so they made their appeal. Jesus' heart went out to these people in their need. His reply was to tell them to go to the priests for the stipulated medical check for those claiming a cure. He did not touch them but challenged them to believe that they were to be cured. They responded by obeying, trusting in his power to heal them, and as they went the miracle took place.

4. The main interest in this story is in how they then reacted. They were already on their way to where they would find the priests for the all-important medical inspection that would lead to their return to life as it had been before. Nine continued their journey, thinking only of the future, but one turned back, full of praise to God and thanks to Jesus. Jesus' comment on the situation showed not just his love and care for them but his sadness at their ingratitude. He noticed that it was the foreigner who had shown his appreciation, while fellow-Jews had taken it all for granted.

OPTIONAL ACTIVITIES

1. Discuss how we feel when "taken for granted". Do we appreciate what others do for us, especially our family? How can we show our appreciation? How can we help newcomers to feel welcome.

2. The class could find out more about leprosy—in history and today. This could be part of a study of various diseases throughout the world.

3. Discuss medical work, including missionaries who care for people in need.

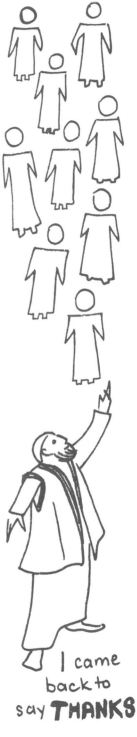

I came back to say **THANKS**

THANK YOU

THE SAYINGS OF JESUS

Jesus said...

I AM....

I CARE

FOLLOW....

I WILL MAKE...

INTRODUCTORY NOTE

This section of the book contains a selection of some well-known sayings of Jesus, giving the reference and, in some cases, the surrounding context as well. It is not intended that teachers should study these altogether in one project but rather that *a few be chosen* according to the age and maturity of the class and talked over in a leisurely atmosphere. They may in fact be spread out over several years; there is so much material and so many different levels of understanding that it is also possible to teach them one session and go over them in another, thus encouraging development in the children's thinking and interpretation. The emphasis is intended to be on Jesus' love, understanding, care and essential interest in the lives of his listeners. Whenever applicable, teach the saying in its situation—Jesus often used the things around him at the moment to drive home his lesson. It might be helpful too (as suggested in Lesson 3) to build up a present-day situation in which to apply the lessons.

The four suggested lessons are:

Jesus says, "I am".
Jesus says, "I care about you".
Jesus says, "Follow my example".
Jesus says, "I will make you strong enough".

Lesson 1   Jesus Says, "I Am"

AIM

To show that Jesus claimed to give true life, understanding and daily care. Older children will see the deeper spiritual parallels to our physical lives.

SHEPHERD

growth

BREAD

SUGGESTED PROCEDURE

1. "I am the gate for the sheep" John 10:7 (verses 7–9)
   "I am the good shepherd" John 10:11 (verses 11–16).
   Find out as much as possible about eastern shepherds and sheep folds in Bible times and put these words into their natural context. The latter were "simple walled enclosures usually without roofs, with the walls covered with thorns to keep out robbers. Several flocks would usually spend the night in one fold under the care of a shepherd who guarded the door" (*Zondervan Pictorial Bible Dictionary*).
   The shepherd knew his own sheep while they in turn recognized his voice. He walked ahead of them, carrying his sling, his rod (cudgel) and his staff (crook), looking for the best pastures.
2. "I am the bread of life" John 6:35 (verses 25–35)
   Jesus said this shortly after he had fed the crowd of more than five thousand people; they had followed him to hear more and no doubt to see further miracles.
   Bread was an essential part of their diet and so it is again natural that Jesus used it as a picture of what he gives to supply a person's deeper

LIGHT

needs. Show the children that he was talking about something at the very centre of a Jewish person's life. Picture "Baker Street" in Jerusalem and tell how bread was baked almost daily in the individual homes of the villagers or tents in the settlements outside. His hearers, therefore, could easily understand his meaning; some did take him literally, however.

3. "I am the light of the world" John 8:12

Introduce by speaking first about light and darkness in the children's own experience, encouraging them to speak of the confusion, fear or even hurt that can arise when they are left in darkness. Discuss different forms of lighting in Bible times (oil lamps of bronze and terracotta; "candles and candlesticks" were more literally "lamps and lampstands"). There was so much more darkness then, with only the moon and stars providing outside light at night. Jesus' words would therefore make an impact; discuss what he meant, explaining that "light" meant "understanding" and "guidance".

OPTIONAL ACTIVITIES

1. Organize small projects in groups on sheep and shepherds, lighting and baking in Bible times. Books of information are readily available, see page vi.

Mount the results of this project work and underneath write the words of Jesus in large letters.

With older children it might be possible also to collect pictures of present-day application to display alongside, e.g. pictures of fighting and confusion showing the need of "a shepherd", ignorance and unhappiness showing the need of "light", etc.

2. Use could be made of Psalm 23, the Shepherd Psalm.

3. Choose other occupations of that time and think of some illustrations that Jesus might have drawn from them. Perhaps he did—he said so much that it could not possibly all be recorded!

block of clay

shape into lamp

with careful supervision fill with meth and fix wick.

knitting activities for 3rd World countries

baking for local old folks' home

candle making for presents.

Lesson 2 Jesus Says, "I Care about You"

AIM

To show that Jesus longs to care for us as individuals. He wants us to trust him implicitly.

SUGGESTED PROCEDURE

1. "Let the children come to me" Mark 10:14 (verses 13–16)

   Paint this picture exactly as it stands in the Bible. It is beautifully simple and so much reveals the essence of Jesus' character. Act it out, having children dress in national costumes representing as many parts of the world as possible. If the teacher thinks it advisable, allow the children to represent contrasting backgrounds also of wealth and poverty. Emphasize the last verse where Jesus embraced and blessed the boys and girls—after scolding the older folk who had tried to send then away.

2. "Hurry down—I must stay in your house today" John 19:5 (verses 1–10)

   The story of Zacchaeus is told in *Start Here* but should be retold now, showing that Jesus' interest is not in crowds but in personalities, even those disliked so intensely by others. Find out about tax gatherers for the Romans in Bible times (see page 85) and place this man in that context. Ask the children for their reactions to Jesus' invitation to the little man. Why did he make it? What did he hope to do for him?

3. "Ask, and you will receive; seek, and you will find; knock and the door will be opened to you" Luke 11:9 (verses 5–13)

   Discuss this in the context of the very human story (verses 5–8) where a man knocks his neighbour up at midnight; an unsociable act! Discuss the statement too in the context of the children's own homes; what things does a good parent give to his/her child? Everything asked for, or just what is considered best for the child? Try to show that if a person honestly trusts God, he may long to possess something (material or otherwise) but asks that God grant his request only if it is good for him—this is a mature concept, perhaps, but easily enough illustrated. (No parent would give a toddler matches however much he wanted them!) Thoughtful pupils will therefore grasp the fact that a negative answer from God is God's best, just as much as a positive one in other circumstances.

4. "Why worry? . . . Look how the wild flowers grow . . . I tell you that not even King Solomon with all his wealth had clothes as beautiful as one of these flowers" Matthew 6:28–29 (verses 24–34)
'Do not be afraid; you are worth much more than many sparrows" Luke 12:7 (verses 6–7)
In these verses Jesus was showing the futility of worrying and further, in the Matthew reference, the impossibility of truly following God while being a slave to possessions at the same time. Find out a little about the flowers and birds that may have been in evidence as Jesus was talking (flax, juniper, lilies, myrtle, narcissi, crocus, rose of Sharon, etc.; sparrow, dove, raven, owl, eagle, etc.). God cares for them and even more for us. So why worry? (verses 31–32). After all, he says, God knows what we need even before we ask him.
This is a difficult lesson for adults! Often children, however, have a very sensible evaluation of "needs" which we tend to lose. Discuss this with older children.

5. "Be quiet! Be still!" Mark 4:39 (verses 35–41)
Jesus' words to the winds and the waves in the storm are famous ones. The story was dealt with in *Start Here* but retell it. Describe the sudden squalls which blew up so frequently in the Sea of Galilee and draw parallels with the stormy circumstances which can rage around us at certain periods of our lives. Some children will already know much about this in their own family situation. Jesus was able to restore calm in the minds of his disciples—as in the storm itself.

OPTIONAL ACTIVITIES

Write out these words of Jesus and round about each mount cartoon pictures (or any other kind of illustration) depicting up-to-date situations where they would be applicable.

Lesson 3   Jesus Says, "Follow My Example"

AIM

To show that Jesus challenges us to live by his standards—as far as is possible.

SUGGESTED PROCEDURE

The following statements or comments demand honest discussion from the children and this is often better achieved by having them talk "through another person". They are less inhibited in saying how someone else might react rather than openly to state what their own actions might be. It would be helpful, therefore, to spend some time inventing a family; teachers should choose the social background which they feel most closely parallel to their particular pupils, but the children should choose names, jobs (if any!), pets and friends as well as describing the home, school, etc. Draw pictures of them, display them and get to know them over a few weeks. This arouses much interest and stimulates good, lively creative writing and thinking—perhaps it should be used in that way first.

At this stage, begin to invent situations in which the children can identify with different people at different times. A particular member of the family comes up against circumstances where some of Jesus' words could be aptly applied, e.g. a ten-year-old boy is persecuted or bullied by another; Jesus said, "Love your enemies"; what then?

Spend time discussing a range of possible reactions and the likely outcome of these; challenge the class to consider

(a) the reasons for Jesus making his statement,

(b) the difficulties of following that through, and

(c) the possible results.

Keep the discussion's objective except perhaps at the very end when the pupils might sometimes be invited to say what they think they would have done.

The following sayings are in no special sequence:

"Love your enemies" Matthew 5:43–44.

"Do not judge others" Luke 6:37–38, but refer also to the amusing picture in Matthew 7:4–5.

"You are like salt for all mankind" Matthew 5:13 and Mark 9:50. Discuss the need for salt in cooking as well as the custom of "eating salt" as a mark of friendship in Eastern countries.

"Forgive seventy times seven" Matthew 18:21–22. In other words, keep on forgiving!

"Love the Lord your God with all your heart, with all your soul, with all your mind and with all your strength. Love your neighbour as you love yourself" Mark 12:30–31 (verses 28–31).

"Pay the Emperor what belongs to the Emperor and pay God what belongs to God" Mark 12:17 (verses 13–17). It will be necessary here to describe some of the background of Roman rule in Galilee.

"It is much harder for a rich person to enter the Kingdom of God than for a camel to go through the eye of a needle" Mark 10:25 (verses 17–27).

Explain that Jesus was referring to our *attitudes* to our possessions and if possible show a picture of a needle's eye gate, e.g. the Jaffa Gate and others in the Jerusalem wall. "Small doors such as this were common features of the gates of ancient cities; humans could pass through easily but large animals, such as camels, had to be unloaded and kneel to get through" *(Zondervan Pictorial Bible Dictionary)*.

OPTIONAL ACTIVITIES

Small groups within the class could dramatize the family situation set by the teacher. While they rehearse, others could quickly write a similar circumstance with reference to another member of the family—or if preferred prepare to dramatize that too. These should be quick, and therefore unpolished, establishing the concept rather than giving rise to further discussion.

Lesson 4 Jesus Says, "I Will Make You Strong Enough"

AIM

To show that Jesus understands our weaknesses.

SUGGESTED PROCEDURE

1. Briefly discuss materials and substances in our surroundings and ask which are the most lasting. Lead the talk round to "rock" as opposed to "sand" or "clay", etc. In this brief conclusion point out that no person can be expected to live as Jesus lived but Jesus can nevertheless make his followers faith like "rock" in spite of natural weakness and fear.

2. "Don't be afraid, it is I" John 6:20 (verses 16–21)
   "Anyone who hears these words of mine and obeys them is like a wise man who built his house on rock" Matthew 7:24 (verses 24–27).
   Note that the two houses here received the same battering from the elements. The first stood firm; the second collapsed.

3. "You are a rock and on this rock foundation I will build my church" Matthew 16:18 (verses 13–18)
   Explain that "church" refers to the people who followed him and not to any building in which they met together. These words were addressed to Peter, a character weak enough to deny knowing Jesus at his crucifixion (Matthew 26:69–75) but transformed into "rock". This is a difficult thought and should be discussed only with a mature class.

OPTIONAL ACTIVITIES

Set a competition in which children write out from memory a selected number of Jesus' sayings (from any section). Alternatively, allow pupils to select one and write it out in decorative writing.

THE EASTER STORY

As with the Christmas story, we shall look at the main events of this well-known account as they may have been viewed by some of the people present at the time.

Lesson 1   Pontius Pilate

Matthew 27; Mark 15; Luke 23; John 18:29

AIM

To retell the Easter story as seen by Pontius Pilate.

INTRODUCTION

Fill in the historical background to the scene: Roman occupation, pockets of Jewish resistance: Jesus, rejected by most of the Jews and viewed by the Romans as a religious fanatic. Pontius Pilate was the Roman governor of Judea from A.D. 26–36 and was an unpopular ruler of the Jews because of his tactless and often cruel leadership. (More details may be found in *Who? What? Where? in the Bible*.)

SUGGESTED PROCEDURE

Retell the story from Pontius Pilate's viewpoint. The main points are:
1. Normally he lived in his palace at Caesarea on the coast but had to go to Jerusalem to keep order during the Feast of the Passover, when Jews gathered to celebrate and zealots took advantage of the crowded conditions to annoy the Romans.
2. He probably had heard of Jesus but took little notice of him until forced to do so by the Jewish leaders who constantly annoyed him and now brought a petition to him.
3. In Jerusalem the Jews have Jesus arrested in the Garden of Gethsemane led by one of his disciples, Judas Iscariot. The traitor leads the men to Jesus in the dim light of the evening.
4. By the time Jesus is led to Pilate he has already been whipped by the mocking soldiers but instead of being bitter at this unjust treatment, he accepts it without protest. The governor is amazed at the calmness of this man who may face a death penalty. Unlike most of the Jewish patriots who had already come before him for judgment, cursing and protesting the justice of their rebellion against Rome, this man seems different. He tells Jesus to speak up for himself and save his life, but this seemingly innocent man tells the Roman leader that he knows that he will die and that Pilate can do nothing to stop it. Pilate is surprised, wondering if this man really knows the power vested in him by Rome!
5. Normally a callous man, Pilate is disturbed to think that the man may really be innocent of any crime known to Rome. Even his wife says that

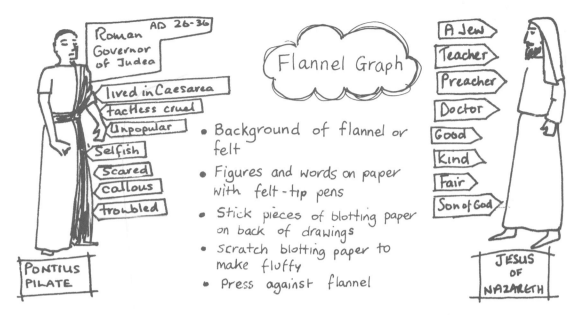

Roman
Governor
of Judea
AD 26-36

lived in Caesarea
tactless cruel
unpopular
selfish
scared
callous
troubled

PONTIUS
PILATE

Flannel Graph

- Background of flannel or felt
- Figures and words on paper with felt-tip pens
- Stick pieces of blotting paper on back of drawings
- Scratch blotting paper to make fluffy
- Press against flannel

A Jew
Teacher
Preacher
Doctor
Good
Kind
Fair
Son of God

JESUS
OF
NAZARETH

she has had sleepless nights thinking about him and Pilate sees an opportunity to have him released. Each year at the Passover a criminal is released as a gesture of appeasement to the Jews, so he offers Jesus to the gathering. To his surprise the crowd demand the release of the murderer zealot, Barabbas.

6. Pilate reluctantly gives in to the demand of the crowd but, as an expression of his continued concern, publicly and symbolically washes his hands of the affair. Jesus is then led away to be crucified.

7. The Roman leader, thinking that this is the end of the story now that the crucifixion has taken place, attempts to put the incident out of his mind.

8. Imagine his consternation at the report that Jesus has been "raised from the dead" and this despite his instruction that a careful guard be put on this man's tomb. He had heard rumours that Jesus had spoken of this but saw it as a cover for the disciples to steal his body. He demands an inquiry and no doubt interviews the soldiers at the cross to verify that he actually died; he speaks perhaps to the soldiers guarding the tomb—had they fallen asleep? Pilate is amazed and probably disbelieves their story of bright lights, etc. Further enquiries speak of sightings, Jesus' followers rejoicing instead of sorrowing and he does his best to dispel rumours but the strange stories persist. He is mystified but gets on with the other tasks he must carry out as governor of this troubled land.

OPTIONAL ACTIVITIES

Have pupils write an account in their own words of the views of Pilate.

1. "Interview" the governor after the resurrection.
2. Explore the contrasting life of the Roman rulers and the Jews in Palestine at this time.
3. Read one of the accounts from the Bible of Pilate's meeting with Jesus.
4. Record one of the noisy scenes at the trial.

Lesson 2   Barabbas

Matthew 27:15–21; Luke 23:18–19

AIM

To tell the Easter story as seen by Barabbas.

INTRODUCTION

Explain that Barabbas was probably a Jewish zealot and a prisoner in Jerusalem at the time of Jesus' arrest and trial. He was probably sentenced to death for his rebellion against the Romans.

SUGGESTED PROCEDURE

Retell the main events of the story as viewed by Barabbas, the main points being:

JESUS

1. Imagine his earlier introduction to a life of crime and of rebellion against the Roman occupation of his country. He viewed himself as a freedom fighter in solidarity with the suffering Jewish people.
2. Build up a picture of his arrest, imprisonment and trial. He may have been captured for example after leading an attack against a Roman foot patrol. He may have heard of Jesus or indeed heard him preaching. Speculate on what he might have thought of Jesus; a religious fanatic perhaps who was wasting his time instead of joining the armed rebellion which disturbed the Romans more.
3. He hears of Jesus' arrest and is probably surprised that the Romans should be concerned about a preacher, although he could understand the concern of the Jewish religious leaders.
4. He knows he will be crucified at the same time as Jesus and feels certain that Jesus will be the one who is given the traditional pardon when he is led for the last time before Pilate and the gathered crowd. Imagine his surprise, his delight and no doubt his measure of shock that the crowd demand *his* release instead of Jesus whom even Pilate says is innocent!

BARABBAS

Newspaper Office

Groups work on
- TRIAL NEWS
- ADVERTS
- RECIPES
- FASHION
- CRIME
- SPORT PAGES.

5. He is released and disappears into the crowd. Does he think of Jesus as the one who saved his life and ask further questions or does he take to the hills grateful for his lucky escape?

OPTIONAL ACTIVITIES

1. Write a poem in Barabbas' own words.
2. Seek him out and "interview" him after his release.
3. Explore further the history of these Jewish "freedom fighters" and discuss the effect they might have had on the Roman rulers. The strength and determination of these people is well illustrated in the account of *Masada* or the *Bronze Bow* by Elizabeth Speare.

Freedom — what it means to me..... ☺ by Barabbas

Lesson 3   Mary Magdalene

John 19:25; John 20

AIM

To recount the story of Easter as told by Mary Magdalene.

INTRODUCTION

Explain that Magdala was a town on the Sea of Galilee. There being more than one Mary in the Bible, this woman was called Mary the Magdalene to distinguish her from the others.

SUGGESTED PROCEDURE

Retell the Easter story as viewed by Mary Magdalene, with these suggested main events:

1. Mary would remember how Jesus had healed her many months before. She had been so impressed by his person and his message that she had followed him with many other disciples as he moved around the country preaching and healing.

bad woman
ill mentally
rejected
despised
CHANGED
healed by Jesus
Forgiven
New Life

Magnetic Board Tin Tray Zinc Plate

Cut out figure from paper. Colour in write words on paper. Fix small strip magnet to back.

Group of children can make up story of Mary Magdalene and tell it to class, using the magnetic board.

MARY

119

2. As one so touched by him she would be surprised that the Jewish religious leaders should hate him so much and would be even more surprised that the Romans had agreed to have him arrested at their request. This is a trumped up charge she is certain and feels sure that the Roman ruler's sense of justice would ensure his release. However she does vaguely remember Jesus' reference to his imminent death as being necessary.

3. Perhaps she mingles with the crowd at his trial and hopes that he will be released at the Passover amnesty gesture. She runs off dismayed and no doubt in tears as Barabbas is given to the crowd, while Jesus is led off like a common criminal to be crucified on a Roman cross. He said he would die but could all this really be happening?

4. In despair she perhaps visits the scene of the crucifixion, vainly hoping for a reprieve.

5. On the first day of the week, the death and burial of Jesus have taken place, Mary goes to the tomb while it is still dark and is dismayed to find that the body has been removed. She runs to tell Peter and John who make their way quickly to the tomb and confirm Mary's story before returning home.

Roman Cross

Model on tray

Papier maché or collection of stone

real stone

pipe cleaner figures dressed. Plasticine

miniature garden

6. Mary, however, remains beside the empty tomb weeping and is surprised by "the gardener" who asks why she is crying. As she replies, "Because they have taken away my Lord and I don't know where they have laid him," she turns round and asks him if he knows anything about it. When Jesus says, "Mary!" she immediately recognizes his voice and gasps his name in surprise. She then runs off to tell the other disciples that she "has seen the Lord".

OPTIONAL ACTIVITIES

1. Interview Mary after the events of the trial and, in contrast, after her experience at the tomb.
2. Teach Easter hymns and carols.
3. Read out the passage from John 20, while others mime the action.
4. Paint or build a collage of different events in Mary's life.
5. Choose another character, e.g. Thomas or a Roman soldier at the cross and look through his eyes as we have done in the preceding lessons.

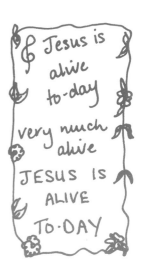

Jesus is alive to-day very much alive JESUS IS ALIVE TO-DAY